ROBERT MUSIL: *An Introduction to His Work*

Robert Musil in his study, Vienna, 1937

ROBERT MUSIL:

An Introduction to His Work

BURTON PIKE

KENNIKAT PRESS
Port Washington, N. Y./London

ROBERT MUSIL

Reissued in 1972 by Kennikat Press by arrangement
Library of Congress Catalog Card No: 75-153236
ISBN 0-8046-1546-2

Manufactured by Taylor Publishing Company Dallas, Texas

FOR

Beatrice Sheridan

Preface

ROBERT MUSIL, who was born in 1880 and died in 1942, is one of those writers whose work seems to gain rather than lose both stature and relevance with the passage of time. In his major works, the play *The Visionaries* and the novel *The Man without Qualities*, Musil addressed himself as an artist with a highly unorthodox conception of art to a basic human problem: How can the individual establish a link between himself and an environment which has less and less place for everything the individual represents?

Musil was an Austrian of the lower nobility. At the close of the nineteenth century and the beginning of the twentieth, to be an Austrian meant to be intensely aware of the fragility and tenuousness of social and political institutions, indeed even habits of thought, which had long outlived a rich and glorious past. At that time, in that place, a thinking person could easily observe and perhaps even feel within himself a dissociation of substance from social values. The gap between the individual and society in the old Austrian Empire was clear. This is the base Musil starts from. By implication he extends the Austrian situation to cover the declining values of Europe in general; more important, he makes out of it a human dilemma not restricted to any geographical area. This dilemma is as follows: The accelerating technology of our time is outrunning more and more the ability of the human mind to adjust to it. Social organizations, patterns of thought, and cherished ideals correspond to a reality that no longer exists; the painful transition to a new and necessary kind of thinking has hardly begun.

The problem of the alienation of the individual and his search for a new, meaningful social context is now emerging clearly as a major pattern in the twentieth-century novel and drama. Thomas Mann's *The Magic Mountain*, Joyce's *Ulysses*, Hermann Broch's *The Sleepwalkers*, Boris Pasternak's *Doctor Zhivago*, and the plays of Bert Brecht are all examples of this pattern. Among those writers concerned with this problem Musil is distinguished by the intellectual brilliance of his conception, his knowledge of the workings of the mind, and his ability to forge language in the crucible of his thought.

Robert Edler von Musil, the son of a professor of engineering at Klagenfurt and Brünn, was destined at an early age for a military career, but changed his mind and studied civil engineering. This did not satisfy him either, and he went to the University of Berlin to study philosophy and experimental psychology, in which he took his degree. When his first novel, *The Confusions of Young Törless*, brought him recognition, he decided against pursuing an academic career in philosophy and in favor of establishing himself as a writer. In 1910 Musil married a woman several years older than himself, with two children by a previous marriage, and took up a position as librarian at the Technical University in Vienna. In 1913 he was called back to Berlin to become one of the editors of the magazine *Die neue Rundschau*. His contributions to that journal, which include among other things a review of Kafka's "The Stoker" ("Der Heizer"), are worthy of a study in themselves.

During the First World War, Musil was an officer in the Austrian army. After the war he worked for a time as a press liaison official in the Austrian War Ministry. From 1922 on he lived as a free-lance writer so that he could devote himself to *The Man without Qualities*. When Germany was closed to him in 1933, Musil found he could no longer support himself. In 1934 a "Musil Society" was formed in Vienna—previously there had been a similar but brief undertaking in Berlin—to provide the writer with financial support.

When the Nazis took over Austria in 1938, Musil left and settled in Switzerland, where he lived until his death four years later. Attempts to interest American organizations in sponsoring Musil's emigration to the United States, although supported by such figures as Albert Einstein and Thomas Mann, failed. Such is the skeletal outline of a life which contained more than the usual measure of drama and suffering.

This book is intended as a critical guide for the general reader and an outline for the scholar. Its aim is modest; it makes no claim to exhaustiveness. In Musil scholarship almost everything remains to be done; the best way to begin seemed to be to secure a general view of the work of this important and difficult writer.

In method the present work is empirical and based closely on the texts. It begins with a short survey of Musil's attitudes toward life and literature and a summary of the characteristics common to his major works of fiction. The aim and scope of this book did not allow for the inclusion of such minor works as the delightful collection of sketches called *Posthumous Papers of a Living Man* (*Nachlass zu Lebzei-*

ten) or the lecture "On Stupidity" ("Über die Dummheit"). Following the summary of characteristics, each of the major works, culminating with *The Man without Qualities*, is examined critically in greater detail.

Many important questions whose answers lie outside the texts are touched on only tangentially, if at all. Among these questions are Musil's debts to Mach, Nietzsche, and German Romanticism and his place in the Austro-German literary tradition.

I would here like to express my gratitude to those who have helped me in the preparation of this work. I owe a special debt of gratitude to a wise and kindly man, Dr. John Kelly, late Emeritus Professor of German at Haverford College, who first awakened my interest in Musil. Professors Henry Hatfield and Harry Levin of Harvard University provided valuable aid while I was preparing the substance of this book as a doctoral dissertation in comparative literature at Harvard. Musil's stepdaughter, the late Mrs. Otto Rosenthal of Philadelphia, and her husband, Dr. Otto Rosenthal, were kind enough to grant me an interview which provided important information. Mr. Walter Grossman of the Harvard College Library, who knew Musil, has also been very helpful.

I am indebted to the following for permission to use copyrighted material: Rowohlt-Verlag for use of the German edition of Musil's works; Coward-McCann and Franz J. Horch Associates for use of the translation by Eithne Wilkins and Ernst Kaiser of *The Man without Qualities* (Vol. I copyright 1953, Vol. II copyright 1954 by Coward-McCann, Inc.); Pantheon Books for material quoted from the English translation of *Young Törless;* the Viking Press for a passage from *The Literary Situation* by Malcolm

Cowley; Harcourt, Brace and World for passages from T. S. Eliot ("The Hollow Men" in *Collected Poems, 1909–1935*, copyright 1936, and "Burnt Norton" and "The Dry Salvages" in *Four Quartets*, copyright 1943); Insel-Verlag for the quotations from Rilke; and the Macmillan Company for a quotation from Yeats's "Oedipus at Colonus" (in *The Collected Poems of W. B. Yeats*, copyright 1928 by the Macmillan Company, renewed 1956 by Georgie Yeats).

Musil's stepson, Professor Gaetano Marcovaldi, was kind enough to provide me with the photograph used for the frontispiece.

BURTON PIKE

Hamburg, 1959
Ithaca, 1961

Contents

I. The Mind of Musil, 1

II. The Fiction of Musil, 11

III. *The Confusions of Young Törless* (1906), 41

IV. *Unions* (1911), 57

V. *The Visionaries* (1921), 71

VI. *Vinzenz and the Girl Friend of Important Men* (1924), 96

VII. *Three Women* (1924), 102

VIII. *The Man without Qualities* (1930–1952), 119

Notes, 201

A Selected Bibliography, 207

Index, 213

ROBERT MUSIL: *An Introduction to His Work*

I

The Mind of Musil

COMBINE the attitudes toward man of Swift, Freud, Nietzsche, Valéry, Shaw, and Bertrand Russell, and the result will roughly delineate the mind of Robert Musil, who was at various times a soldier, an engineer, a philosopher, an experimental psychologist, a librarian, an editor, a dramatic critic, a consultant on military education, and, finally, "nothing but a writer." The detective Stader in Musil's play *The Visionaries* (*Die Schwärmer*) speaks for his creator when he remarks that "one has in oneself something that cannot find satisfaction in any profession. A restlessness of the spirit, I'd say. A final conviction is lacking."[1] And yet far from being external to his writing, all of these activities enriched it, and at the same time do much to explain why Musil's perspective and frame of reference were so largely nonliterary. Musil looked at the world from the viewpoint of a scientific philosopher; he was concerned with analyzing and criticizing the world as it is, and he was more interested in ideas than in actions. His talent, in other words, was analytic and conceptual rather than synthetic and dramatic. In this respect Musil differs considerably from his contemporaries Joyce and Proust, with whom he has been—perhaps rashly—compared.

A rare analytical ability was indeed the leading quality of this "man without qualities." Musil dissected with the scalpel of a glittering, diamond-hard intellect man's behavior and the world he lives in. Real people and actual situations were for him only materials from which to extract an abstract thought or a theoretical organizing principle; this is the limitation of his art as art. (One is reminded by way of contrast of Proust's acid comment that "a book in which there are theories is like an article from which the price mark has not been removed.") [2] "What I care about," Musil wrote in his diary in 1910, "is the passionate energy of thought. Where I can't work out some particular thought, work becomes immediately boring to me; this is true of almost every single paragraph." [3] And the creation of a Baron de Charlus or a Natasha Rostov was equally impossible for a man who looked at the individual *sub specie aeternitatis:* "Disparate in human life are neither the data nor the inner conditions, but their organization in time and space. [The] individual is a derivation (*ein Ablauf*), a variation. Finished with its death. . . . Men are also only variations of a few recurrent types. Even modern men." [4]

Another of Musil's qualities, one which follows from his intellectual orientation, was a profound and thorough skepticism. Like Swift, Nietzsche, and Shaw, Musil showed little empathy with the ordinary inhabitants of the globe, but in his case too this superficial lack of sympathy covered a deeper concern. Unlike Swift and Shaw, but rather like Goethe, Musil probed mankind with a purely intellectual irony, sometimes gentle but always insistent, under which his passion lay partly hidden. In common with other skeptics, Musil was much better at analyzing and criticizing man as he is than at deciding what man ought to be. This deficiency is perhaps inherent in the skeptical mind, for the skeptic, antagonistic as he is to fanaticism of any kind, hesitates to set up an absolute scale of values with its contradictory implication of one standard valid for all. This perhaps explains Musil's vagueness in stating just what the new synthesis he aspired to was to be. Anyone who has patiently followed him through *The Man without Qualities* (*Der Mann ohne Eigenschaften*) is bound to feel that the ideal announced there of a fusion between "exactitude and soul" [5] —a twentieth-century attempt to bridge the Kantian abyss between *Geist* and *Natur*—is somehow an inadequate answer to the problems raised in the book.

If intellectual skepticism were the extent of Musil's talent his place in modern European literature would be small indeed. But like Swift and Nietzsche before him, and his contemporary Shaw, Musil possessed besides a rare analytical ability the quality of moral indignation—without, however, Swift's rancor or Shaw's explosiveness—at the discrepancy between what man is and what he ought to be as the only creature capable of rationality. Musil often reduces this problem to the more immediate level of the discrepancy between what man could do and what he does.

Noting that there is a type of man who is aesthetically sensitive, Musil placed himself in an opposite camp: "I am morally sensitive," he said; [6] and the need for a new morality to correspond to the rapid advances in technology of the twentieth century is the central point of his forty-year labor of love, *The Man without Qualities.* Indeed Musil's whole conception of fiction is a moral one. In "Theoretical Observations on the Life of a Writer" ("Theoretisches zu dem Leben eines Dichters"), a series of notes tentatively dated 1936, Musil wrote:

It is not the task of fiction (*Dichtung*) to depict that which is, but that which ought to be; or that which could be, as a partial solution of that which ought to be. . . . Fiction is living ethic. Usually a depiction of moral exceptions. But also from time to time a summing up of the morality of exception. Here all the questions are joined: fiction and perfect state, fiction and action, fiction and politics. The position of exception and the importance of the writer.[7]

But for reasons which will shortly become apparent, Musil's moral sense needs to be rather carefully described. Generally speaking, it is humanistic, and rests on the conviction that man can improve himself, or that a person has the potential to realize himself more fully than he does. "Become what it is in you to be" might be taken as Musil's categorical imperative, and the attempt to fulfill such a command can be seen in the major characters of all his works. This is the point at which Musil most closely approaches the imperious exhortations of Nietzsche and the reflective humanism of Gide. For Musil, man is morally responsible for his acts. If man is crushed by modern life, it is not the complexity of civilization which has ground him under its wheel, but rather his own inability to keep up psychologically with a rapidly changing world. "The fault, dear Brutus, is not in our stars but in ourselves, that we are underlings." It follows that Musil's concern was with the individual and not with the mass, and this orientation toward the individual is of prime importance in his work.

Like all morality, Musil's rests on a tacit standard of values; the assertion that this or that is "wrong" with a person's attitude toward the world is itself a value judgment. One might say generally that the world presented in a novel, as an analogue or heightened picture of the external world, involves by definition some system of moral valuation. But especially in Musil's case morality should not be confused with religious morality. It is axiomatic that a moral sense and Christian morality, for example, can be very different things. As Voltaire demonstrated, good skeptics make poor Christians, and Musil was no exception to the rule. There is more to the absence of a specifically Christian God and a specifically Christian morality from Musil's outlook, I think, than the enlightened rationalism of his parents can account for. ("My parents were for enlightenment in every respect," he once wrote.[8]) We must here bear in mind not only Musil's thorough skepticism, but also his rigorous training as an empirical scientist. Religion was for him simply one manifestation of human activity, on a plane with science and art, and like them subordinate to thought. Especially significant in this connection is the tone of the following diary entry, written while Musil was sick in bed and reading *Anna Karenina:*

It occurred to me: to represent a man who grew up under Christian morality, and to investigate whether he comes to mine. But do I have one? (Don't forget to incorporate this Christian morality softly, undogmatically and lovably in a mother one can love.) I believe I don't have a morality. Reason: everything becomes for me fragments of a theoretical system. But I have given up philosophy, thus there is no justification for it. There remain only: illuminations.[9]

Note that Musil is here talking about a systematic personal morality, not an ideal one; indeed, the conflict between the two forms an important tension in his thought.

Restlessness, analysis, skepticism, morality; in Musil's thought all these qualities are centered on one key word: *Möglichkeit.* Raskolnikov was no more obsessed with his crime than was Musil with this fatal word, "possibility." It occurs significantly in every one of his works, and always in the same connection: a self-conscious character who is trying to adjust his inner life of feeling to the increasingly impersonal reality of twentieth-century urban life (this is one of several areas in which Musil comes close to Rilke, his favorite poet) suddenly realizes that what he is doing does not make any difference. He could just as well have done it differently, or done something else. Life offers to the individual, at any given moment or as a whole, unlimited possibilities. Any action is a choice among possibilities, and, in Musil's view, is no more valid than the unrealized alternatives. Musil the scientist sees them as all equally valid; his scientific relativism sometimes approaches relativistic paralysis. "There are truths," he wrote at the age of twenty-two, "but no truth. I can quite well maintain two things completely opposed to each other, and be right in both cases." [10]

But Musil the moralist founders on this iceberg whose implications lie hidden beneath the surface. For to a behavioral scientist, morality is irrelevant; he is interested in modes and patterns of behavior which simply exist, and tries to place each individual action within the pattern of its conditioning influences. The verb "ought" does not concern him; to his consistent logical mind it seems ridiculous to label an action good or bad, right or wrong, for all actions can be explained, or at least described, in rational terms. Thus from a logical point of view a scientific moralist would seem to be a contradiction in terms: the scientist does not judge, the moralist does. This paradox makes the foundation of Musil's new morality somewhat shaky; a *fusion* of "exactitude and soul" is a very different process from using exactitude as a tool with which to pry open the soul like a reluctant oyster—which, in *The Man without Qualities*, Musil seems to be attempting to do. And yet one of Musil's major contributions is that he illuminated this basic paradox of our time so strongly.

One of the most insistent themes in *The Man without Qualities* is that life offers the individual unlimited possibilities. This is, at least by implication, something positive. For life is open and indifferent, Musil seems to feel, and the rare person who is aware of this openness and indifference is somehow superior to the individual whose horizons are automatically closed by his "dedication" to a cause. From this point of view there is more merit in detachment than in attachment. But the fact remains that Musil himself, like Ulrich, the protagonist of *The Man without Qualities*, fell victim to the siren of possibility. Life paralyzed them both. They tried many things, and did many of them well, but did not have the capacity to commit themselves to one thing. "The world was all before them, where to choose," but they had no image of Eden, no fixed point of reference to anchor them to life. Musil described both himself and Ulrich as *Möglichkeitsmenschen,* men of possibility; the term is an admission of insufficiency. Both Musil and Ulrich had many positive qualities, but lacked the ability to act directly and unself-consciously which translates qualities from thought to action and thus gives them value. Concern over this lack seems to lie behind Musil's complaint that in the modern world material relationships have superseded human ones. "A world of qualities without man has arisen," [11] exclaims Ulrich at one point and, even closer to the core of Musil's thought: "In earlier times one had a better conscience about being a person than one does today." [12]

To be aware of the possibilities of life to a degree approaching paralysis indicates that one stands apart from the main stream of life and that one has, at least in some degree, an attitude of emotional and intellectual detachment from society. That Musil was a solitary man is therefore not surprising. Especially after the First World War he lived and worked in seclusion. According to his stepdaughter Musil's only close friend was Franz Blei.[13] It would, however, be inaccurate to call Musil lonely, for besides having an unusually close relationship with his wife he was a man of independent and self-sufficient mind. Although he often complains of the world's nonrecognition of his talent, the reader of his diaries feels that he derived a grim satisfaction from toiling in obscurity for the sake of the future. The "future" kept him going for forty years, through war, peace, and grinding poverty, working on *The Man without Qualities.* In "Thoughts for a 'Foreword' " to this novel Musil wrote: "I dedicate this novel to German youth. Not that of today—mental vacuum after the [First] War—quite amusing rogues—but to the youth which will come some time hence, and which will have to begin precisely where we stopped before the war." [14] And often elsewhere Musil, like Stendhal before him, expresses with confidence the opinion that his sacrifices in life will be fully justified not in the next world, but in the future development of this one.

In an essay on Musil one critic, Gert Kalow, advances as a reason for Musil's social asceticism the idea that he regarded himself as embarking on voyages of discovery toward new continents of the possibilities of life.[15] This makes one think of Musil stepping onto the steamer in one of Baudelaire's poems, about to sail for exotic lands—and in his last years, Kalow informs us, Musil did carry around with him a visa for China, not intending to go there, but simply as a "secret patent of citizenship."[16] However this may be, a more concrete force behind Musil's isolation was his impatience with simplistic attitudes in others. Precisely on this account he dissociated himself from the expressionist movement,[17] and his frequent biting remarks about distinguished contemporaries indicate strikingly his skepticism and the independence of his judgment.

Indeed, Musil's self-sufficiency in isolation was extraordinary; the only comparable case, perhaps, is that of Thoreau, with whose writings Musil seems to have been acquainted. This self-sufficiency must be accounted a drawback in certain respects. It seems to have led to too great an application of Musil's analytic powers to his own personality, and at the same time to too little understanding of other people as differently constituted individuals. But with his perceptive clarity Musil saw that there was in his isolation perhaps something deeper than the impatience of a skeptic with the obtuseness of others: a deep-rooted opposition to life itself, which finds occasional expression in his works and diaries.[18] In a sense, *The Man without Qualities* might be taken as Musil's vicarious attempt to come out of his corner and rejoin the human race. His obsession in that novel with the isolation of man in the modern world can be taken in part at least as a rationalization of his own situation.

Enough has been said so far to indicate in a general way the extraordinary complexity and peculiar perspective of this champion of the intellect. To this should be added some indication of the remarkable extent of his knowledge. The best idea of this wide scope can be obtained, I think, by turning to the Index to Volume Two of the Rowohlt edition of his collected works, *Diaries, Aphorisms, Essays, and Addresses* (*Tagebücher, Aphorismen, Essays und Reden*). One finds there, immediately after Aeschylus and St. Francis of

Assisi, Kemal Ataturk. Aubrey Beardsley, William Blake, Boccaccio, Böcklin, and Botticelli are followed at a respectful distance by Emily Brontë, La Bruyère, Buddha, and Byron; Carlyle has six entries to Hans Carossa's one; Enrico Caruso, Cervantes, the two Chamberlains (Houston Stewart and Neville), and William Ellery Channing form a series of strange bedfellows, perhaps outdone by the eleven immediately following them: Charlie Chaplin, G. K. Chesterton, Chiang Kai-shek, Winston Churchill, Count Ciano, Cicero, René Clair, Claudel, Clausewitz, Clemenceau, and Colette. Of special interest are the eleven entries devoted to Ralph Waldo Emerson; William Faulkner is also mentioned. Musil had a great deal to say about Stefan George, Goethe, Hitler, Ibsen, Kant, Karl Kraus, Thomas Mann, Mussolini, Napoleon, Nietzsche (fifty-four entries), Rilke, Tolstoy, Wagner, and Werfel. Pitirim Sorokin, Franklin Roosevelt, Swedenborg, and Swinburne are also present. This random sampling will sufficiently indicate the complexity of the man and the range of the work.

In presenting even in broad strokes an impression of this protean mind, one feels rather like the "belated literary geologist" in one of Musil's whimsical sketches. This man comes up to Musil, who is sitting in the landscape of his own brain, and starts discussing the author's works: "From time to time [the geologist] spat . . . in front of himself into a small tender fold of the Musilian cerebral cortex, and rubbed it in with his foot." [19] We might say of Musil what the Countess Leonore says of Tasso in Goethe's play *Torquato Tasso:* "His mind gathers up that which is widely scattered." But whether the following line is applicable—"And his feeling inspires the inanimate"—will be examined in later chapters.

~ II ~

The Fiction of Musil

MUSIL'S creative work was produced over a period of some forty years, much of which was devoted exclusively to writing. It consists principally of two novels, two stories, three novellas, one play, and one farce. A brief résumé of each, emphasizing the less familiar shorter works, will set the stage for a discussion of some general principles behind the work as a whole.

Musil's first novel, *The Confusions of Young Törless* (*Die Verwirrungen des Zöglings Törless*) (1906), concerns the reactions of a sensitive adolescent boy to the cruelty of warped fellow students at a military school. The emphasis in this impressive book is on the self-realization to which Törless is forced as a result of the experiences which he witnesses and in which he is psychologically implicated. Through this self-realization Törless grows up and becomes ready to face life. In the body of Musil's work *Törless* stands somewhat apart in its single-minded focus on its protagonist and in the relative simplicity and directness of its narrative style.

Törless, which launched Musil's literary career, was one of a number of novels about school life (*Schulromane*) which were popular in German-speaking countries shortly after the turn of the present century. The American work closest to these novels is J. D. Salinger's *The Catcher in the Rye;* the contrast between it and *Törless* is illuminating. They are markedly different treatments of the same theme, the sensitive adolescent trying to come to terms with himself and society.

Unions (*Vereinigungen*) appeared five years after *Törless.* The first of these two stories, "The Completion of Love" ("Die Vollendung der Liebe"), follows the succession of half-conscious emotions in a woman who leaves her husband for a few days to visit her daughter, and who is seduced by a bearded stranger. The second, "The Temptation of the Silent Veronika" ("Die Versuchung der stillen Veronika"), is an obscure story in which sexual repression on the part of the hero and heroine block a marriage to which there are, as far as one can tell, no external obstacles. Claudine, in "The Completion of Love," is distinctly related to the nymphomaniac Bonadea in the later novel, while Veronika, the heroine of the second story, seems to be the demonic Clarisse at an early stage of crystallization.

The title *Vereinigungen* is to be understood, I think, in a metaphysical as well as a literal sense. The unions in both cases are moments of psychological illumination which result from similar processes. In both stories a woman is physically separated from the man who is the object of her love, in the first story at the beginning, in the second near the end. This leads to a new consciousness on the part of the heroine of her own identity, which has been long submerged and almost forgotten in daily contact with the male protagonist. Through the presence of a second man as catalyst in each case, this brings about a psychological revelation to the heroine about herself. The process is the same as that summed up by Eliot in a different context in *Four Quartets:* "We had the experience but missed the meaning, / And approach to the meaning restores the experience / In a different form."

The drama *The Visionaries* (*Die Schwärmer*) was published in 1921, ten years after *Unions.* The hero of the play, Thomas, is the first significant example in Musil's works of that fateful type, the man of possibility. He is at once a symbol for the author and for reflective man in the modern world in general. The action in this scintillating play is of the slightest; the emphasis is rather on a network of tangled psychological relationships which are presented in a series of sharp verbal duels. The two male principals are opposite types. Thomas is a scientist—as are almost all Musil's male protagonists—successful, rational, and with a detached view of life. He is the type of the almost-ideal man neutralized in human relationships by his too-comprehensive thought. Anselm, who is something like Marchbanks in Shaw's *Candida,* is a failure, a liar, a coward, and a cheat. And yet even after Anselm has been exposed, Maria, Thomas' large and impressive wife, still decides to abandon her husband for Anselm. Anselm has at least warmth enough to arouse her emotionally, she maintains, while her husband's constitutional coolness leaves her cold. The two women in the play, Maria and her sister Regine, are at once the judges and the prizes of a battle which is fought on rational grounds between Thomas, Anselm, and Josef, Regine's husband. But the women appeal from logically demonstrated rational arguments to their own spontaneous feelings; Eros, Musil's favorite god, carries the day.

The farce *Vinzenz and the Girl Friend of Important Men* (*Vinzenz und die Freundin bedeutender Männer*) of 1924 is the slightest of Musil's major works. It is a comic version of *The Visionaries*, whose action it repeats on a lower plane. Vinzenz, an insurance actuary, and Alpha, the "girl friend" of the title, are kindred spirits. In Thomas' terms they are "people without feeling," who shock the other characters by their detached attitudes and amoral actions. In this work too the erotic plays a large role.

Three Women (*Drei Frauen*), which also appeared in 1924, consists of three novellas, "Grigia," "The Portuguese Lady" ("Die Portugiesin"), and "Tonka." In "Grigia," as in "The Completion of Love," the story is set in motion by separation, in this case that of the geologist Homo from his wife and sick son. He is called to work in a primitive region of Italy. There, driven by an obscure death-wish among the wild, sexually free natives—who were originally of German origin—Homo has an affair with a cowgirl whom he nicknames Grigia; her real name is Lena Maria Lenzi. (Musil's heroes have a curious knack of rebaptizing women with pseudosymbolic names; thus in *The Man without Qualities* Ulrich ironically transforms with this magic wand a nymphomaniac into "Bonadea" and Ermelinda Tuzzi, the wife of a government official, into "Diotima.") Eventually Homo is imprisoned by Grigia's jealous husband and left to starve. While the minute depiction of landscape and people in this story recalls Stifter's *Stones of Many Colors*, the progressive deterioration of Homo's mental state roughly parallels that of Gustav von Aschenbach in Thomas Mann's *Death in Venice*.

"The Portuguese Lady," on the other hand, is reminiscent of Tieck and Hawthorne, and might be compared to such modern works as Heimito von Doderer's "The Last Adventure." Aside from "Veronika," this work of rare beauty is by all odds Musil's most peculiar story. It is also the only one of his works not set in the present day. The Portuguese lady is brought home to a cold and forbidding world in northern Italy as the bride of a feudal lord, Herr von Ketten. She remains a shadowy figure, while her husband is the only really strong and active character to be found in Musil's works. After some years this valiant warrior is robbed of his strength by a fever, but eventually recovers. As he does, a mysterious godlike cat sickens and dies, and the lord and his wife are spiritually united.

The third story in this collection, "Tonka," is, in contrast to "The Portuguese Lady," mundane. Here again two nationalities meet, in this case Czech and German. The unnamed hero is a scientist and an inquisitive cultured man of the middle class. He falls in love with Tonka, a lower-class Czech girl of the Gretchen variety and a prime example of a phenomenon rare in Musil's writings, inarticulateness (Grigia is another). On Tonka's account the man breaks with his family, and lives with her for two years. When Tonka becomes pregnant, he believes for certain reasons that he is not responsible; she keeps silent and dies. Like Törless, the hero goes on to become better for having been through a soul-trying and potentially destructive experience. "Tonka" is the only one of Musil's writings with an aura of *fin-de-siècle* decadence. One is reminded of Schnitzler's "Dying" and similar stories.

Common to all the stories in *Three Women* is a marginal setting in which two different nationalities blend and clash. They also share the principle of the outsider, a person from a different country or class who impinges on another character's consciousness, dissolves its patterns of thought and behavior, and brings about a reorientation. All three women are passive agents in their respective stories; they precipitate crises for the men who are attracted to them. These crises lead to death in "Grigia," to life and reconciliation in "The Portuguese Lady," and to life through a sacrificial death in "Tonka."

In *The Man without Qualities*, an unfinished encyclopedic novel which preoccupied Musil for most of his creative life, Ulrich, a man in his thirties, takes a year off to decide what to do with his life. The year is 1913–1914; the locale is the old Austrian Empire, a world in which "from one roof to another would have taken an eagle only a few wing-strokes; but to the modern soul, which playfully bridges oceans and continents, nothing is as impossible as finding the link to those souls who live around the next corner."[1] A close analogue of Valéry's Monsieur Teste, and like him an antihero, Ulrich's overdeveloped cerebral cortex is paralyzed by the possibilities of life; he is a man of possibility with a vengeance. Ulrich finally withdraws from the world entirely, an act symbolized by his turning to his sister Agathe, his mental twin. She is the only person who understands him and whom he understands, in spite of the powerful antagonism to which their likeness gives rise. Their incestuous relationship sets the seal on Ulrich's denial of the world, although he later returns to society. Interwoven with Ulrich's "story" (the term implies narrative action, which receives no emphasis in this enormous work) is a probing satire on the governing aristocracy and business circles of the old Austrian Empire. This broadens into a searching analysis of the human condition and what might be termed the *malheur d'être homme* in a Pascalian sense, the final intellectual misery of a man who realizes the limitations of the situation of the human being. The atmosphere of this novel is that of the clear dry desert air of reflective thought; its almost clinical language is far from a dramatic or lyric view of life.

What are some of the general characteristics of this body of writing, whose form is more diverse than its content? As a whole, Musil's fiction might best be characterized as *Ideendichtung*, a poesy of ideas. (I am using "poesy" here as the closest equivalent in English to *Dichtung*.) Goethe once said in one of his aphorisms that "to live in the idea means to treat the impossible as if it were possible." [2] This is not only the way in which Musil looks at his characters; it is the way in which his characters look at life. The characters live either in their own ideas and feelings or in an abstracted precipitate of those current in the world around them. What and how they *think* and *feel* is always at the center of Musil's novels, stories, and plays; with few exceptions, deeds in his works are so laden with psychological introspection that they lose the name of action.

The primary orientation of *Ideendichtung* is, I would say, toward the general idea underlying an individual problem or attitude. While this orientation is challenging and fruitful in the hands of a writer as talented as Musil, it tends to produce at times, even in his writings, a preoccupation with theory at the expense of the work. That Musil was aware of the dangers in his theoretical approach to literature is shown by such solemn warnings to himself as this one, noted in the Vienna railroad station in 1911 while he was waiting for his wife to arrive from Rome:

One must never lose oneself in the deduction of ideas; that is preparatory work. One should put the ideas—which have gradually closed themselves into a unified circle—into the mouths of the characters, or he should let the characters act from such ideas or in illustration of them. But one must (this is the certain mischief of it) rather take something away from the idea and its consequences and eventualities than sacrifice the liveliness and practical possibility of the situation.[3]

And in the same vein, but even stronger: "Just reach into full human life, and wherever you seize it, it's interesting: this warning tablet [from Goethe's *Faust*] has really been put up for me! Always begin with the concrete! With the effortless letting the ideas come! Never from the idea! Otherwise you brake to a stop immediately."[4] Unfortunately or otherwise, these warnings were often of little effect.

Musil's emphasis on presenting his characters by showing the succession of their mental impressions has naturally led his readers to conclude that the core of his work is psychological. This Musil emphatically, if not too effectively, denies. In denying the charge, however, he makes the point that "what passes for psychology in a work of literature is something other than psychology, just as literature is something other than science, and the indiscriminate use of the word has, like every important equivocation, already had confusing consequences."[5]

I think it is apparent from what has been said so far that the essential subject matter of Musil's fiction is not the psychological, sociological, or political themes, however important they may at first seem, but the process of an individual searching for an ideal balance between himself and the world, or more specifically between his inner and outer selves. None of Musil's major characters ever find this balance, although the conclusions of both *Törless* and "Tonka" indicate that the protagonists of these works will achieve it at some indefinite future time. Törless, in making his "confession" before the school authorities, breaks through the wall of introspective passivity to perform an action which is courageous and meaningful—for him. It is misunderstood and underestimated by the "world." None of Musil's protagonists succeeds in establishing real contact between his inner and the outer world, each of which exists for itself. In Musil's works the realm of inner existence is the higher reality; like the school in *Törless,* the external world usually remains sketchily peripheral, the source of sensory impressions and social action for the characters. But it is on the inner workings of the sensory mechanisms and the reactions produced by them in the form of feelings and ideas that Musil's powerful microscope is focused. In *The Man without Qualities* a further dimension is added: inner existence is looked at not impressionistically, as in *Unions,* but from a generally detached, clinical viewpoint.

Musil's protagonists call to mind Rilke's lines, "Und mit kleinen Schritten gehen die Uhren / Neben unserm eigentlichen Tag" ("And with little steps the clocks walk beside our *real* day").[6] Whatever may happen to them in later years, when the works in which they figure end, Musil's major characters are almost pitifully bewildered by their failure to reconcile their inner and outer lives. Life has defeated them, and they might all sigh, with Thomas in *The Visionaries,* that dreamers like himself have a quality not shared by the mass of human beings: "A sinking at every moment down through everything into the bottomless. Without perishing. The creative condition."[7] This "creative condition" is cold comfort for a man like Ulrich who concludes that "a whole man no longer stands against a whole world, but a human something moves in a diffuse culture medium."[8]

The dichotomy between the inner and the outer life is reflected in the areas of life on which Musil chose to concentrate in his fiction. In a section of one of his diaries entitled "The Theater and Novel of Illusion" ("Illusionstheater und -roman") he singles out social and erotic experience as the two cardinal areas of operation for the dramatist and novelist. These symbolize "experiences that everyone can have, but doesn't."[9] And these are the loci around which the ellipses of Musil's works revolve. Both social and erotic experience are primary means of individual expression, and a person's identity is largely determined by his position in regard to his inner existence (of which the erotic is the most personal area) and to his outer, social life. This dichotomy between the inner and the outer life is sharpest in *The Man without Qualities*, but it is basic to the characters in all Musil's works. Whether this split is as well defined in life as Musil maintains is a moot point, but in his writing it does serve a valuable mechanical function: it focuses his ideas and orders the encyclopedic mass of material which, in *The Man without Qualities*, is almost overwhelming.

In view of Musil's whole abstract orientation toward fiction it is natural that external action in his works is minimized. Action is minimized in his shorter works, and sometimes replaced entirely, by an impressionistic depiction of successive mental states. In the fiction written between his two novels Musil's usual technique is to proceed by a subtle association of feelings in the mind of a character on a semiconscious plane. This unorthodox but effective procedure, in which the reader often finds himself baffled rationally but responding emotionally, reaches its most extreme point in Musil's writings in "The Temptation of the Silent Veronika." Thereafter, and especially in *The Man without Qualities*, Musil gives only the results of these associative processes of feeling in his characters. The sea of inner life is seen from a somewhat greater distance in the later novel; clarity and rationality predominate in this work, and "essayism" displaces impressionism. Essayism, by no means original with Musil, is a suspension of the action of a work by a general, impersonal discussion of a point brought up in the course of the work. For Musil, essayism was of prime importance; it was, as the reader of his diaries will notice, the way in which his mind worked. There is a fascinating essay on essayism in *The Man without Qualities* (Book I, Chapter 62) in which Musil says that "an essay is the unique and unchangeable form which the inner life of a person assumes in a crucial thought."[10]

In "Theoretical Observations on the Life of a Writer" Musil explains how, of the many ways of representing the psychology of the individual, he hit in *Unions* on what he calls the " 'maximally laden path' (the path of the smallest steps), the path of the most gradual, least noticeable transition. That has a moral value: the demonstration of the moral spectrum with the constant transitions from something to its opposite." This leads to a further principle, that of the " 'motivated step.' . . . Its rule is: Let nothing happen (or: do nothing) that is not spiritually (*seelisch*) valuable. This means also: Do nothing causal, do nothing mechanical."[11] It is evident that these principles, applied to a poesy of ideas and mental processes in which action is minimized, are a severe limitation of Musil's art. They substitute for action a highly intellectualized and static imagery of thought and feeling. The metaphor of Zeno's arrow is especially relevant for Musil, in much of whose work the arrow is stopped in each minute "unit" of its flight and thoroughly examined, with the result that the flight itself is barely perceptible. Happily, Musil's theoretical principles are somewhat diluted in practice.

On the one hand, then, Musil's psychological orientation was obviously toward the theoretical rather than the concrete, toward the typical and general rather than the particular and individual. On the other hand his works show an intense preoccupation with the fates of individual people. What is at stake in the cosmic game is not a general principle, but Törless' life, Thomas' life and Ulrich's life. Much of the intensity of this preoccupation seems due to autobiographical forces, as the quotations from Musil's diaries and notes in this book indicate; but whatever its source, this conflict in Musil's works between the general and the individual is a central paradox. The tension which springs from this paradox gives Musil's writing heartbeat and pulse.

But the heart itself lies deeper than the paradox. I think it is to be found in a kind of fear underlying the articulation and articulateness of the work, a Pascalian sense of the dread silence above and beneath the chatter of mankind. In a way the most interesting phenomenon in all Musil's works is not what is said, but what is not said or only half articulated; Törless' confession, Thomas' final broken speech, Claudine's feeling for her husband, Tonka's enigmatic silence, Ulrich's deep awareness of the chasm in which he moves. In these silences or stammered speeches Musil's characters are most intensely individual. The framework of articulateness which surrounds these silences and stammerings makes the characters more general and typical; here the brilliant intellect is at work attempting to rationalize the irrational, to find some pattern or formula of order which will reconcile man and the universe.

The orientation of Musil's fiction toward feelings and ideas suggests some of the problems raised by this approach to literature. The most basic of these problems deserves special emphasis. The reader of any of Musil's works will at once be struck by its impersonality; this is true even of his diaries. But this impersonality is a surface quality; underlying it is a strong passion, and the tension which these two forces create is evident both in Musil and in his work. Speaking of *The Man without Qualities* in an interview in 1926, Musil said: "The real explanation of real happenings doesn't interest me. My memory is bad. Besides, facts are always interchangeable. What interests me is the spiritually typical, I might even say: the ghostliness of action." [12] Thirteen years earlier Musil had noted in passing (insofar as his penetrating eye ever noted anything "in passing"): "How far from literature the inner life, ambition, happiness, spirituality, etc. of our time takes place." [13] So far so good; one might say that Musil was simply explaining his bias as a writer. But he insisted too much and too often on the suppression of the personal element. Although most of his work contains prominent autobiographical traces, Musil insisted on his distance from his subject matter, or, in other words, on his emotional detachment from it. In the fragment "Testament II" (1932?) he wrote:

I felt [while writing] strong resistance against telling about myself, although I had to resolve to do it; but thus it begins to interest me, since it is new even to me—This writer is highly indifferent toward his material. There are writers who are seized by a subject; they feel: with this or none. It is like love at first sight. The relationship of R.M. to his subjects is a hesitant one. He has several at the same time, and keeps them with him after the hours of first love are past, or even without their having been there at all. He capriciously interchanges parts of them. . . . He apparently holds the external to be more or less indifferent.[14]

A specific instance of how scrupulously Musil insisted on an impersonal style in his fiction is shown by the following diary entry, dated 1910:

In "Claudine" ["The Completion of Love"] it cannot go: somewhere a clock began to speak with itself about time, steps walked, etc.—that is lyricism. It must go: a clock struck, Claudine felt it as if somewhere were beginning . . . steps walked, etc.—in the first case the author is saying through the selection of the image itself: how pretty, he emphasizes that it should be pretty, etc. Maxim: the author should show himself only in the ministerial accoutrements of his characters. He should always put the responsibility on them. That is not only more clever, but it is by means of that that, remarkably, the epic arises.[15]

Musil himself stated the paradox of his approach to literature succinctly (it is implicit in almost everything he wrote) in his definition of literature as "a boldly, logically combined life. A production or deductive analysis of possibilities, etc. It is a fervor that consumes the flesh down to the bone for an intellectually emotional goal." [16] An *intellectually* emotional goal—there is in Musil a consistent refusal to recognize emotion as a valid quality in itself, an insistence on the superiority of the intellect. But Musil's passionate concern for his Törless, his Thomas, his Ulrich, and ultimately himself undercuts the too often and too strongly stated attitude of detachment toward his material. Like a towering quiescent volcano Musil seems to cover his upper slopes with snow in a vain attempt to cool the fires burning within. Precisely this polarity makes Musil's fiction come alive. The extreme tension between the personal and the impersonal seizes the reader's imagination. It arises perhaps from the fact that Musil lived in his writing. His personal life stands very much in the background; he did not pour his energy into brilliant letters or diaries, or extensive social intercourse. He held himself largely aloof from the bright world of Vienna, and after the early twenties withdrew almost entirely into *The Man without Qualities*. More, I think, than is the case with any other modern European writer, the expression of Musil the man is to be found in his work.

The conflict between the individual and the world is emphasized in Musil's writings in a very curious way. Except for the first story of *Unions*, the titles of all his works involve personal characteristics. In addition, the titles of his two novels focus on individuals: *The Confusions of Young Törless* and *The Man without Qualities* are thus consistent in this respect with "The Temptation of the Silent Veronika," *The Visionaries*, *Vinzenz and the Girl Friend of Important Men*, and *Three Women* ("Grigia," "The Portuguese Lady," "Tonka"). A look at the openings of the novels is revealing. For purposes of comparison, let us first look at the openings of two other contemporary novels. The first sentence of Kafka's *The Castle* is: "It was late in the evening when K. arrived"; and Mann's *The Magic Mountain* begins: "A simple young man traveled in the summer from Hamburg, his native city, to Davos-Platz in the Graubund. He was going for a visit of three weeks." Here, on the other hand, is how *The Confusions of Young Törless* begins: "It was a small station on the long railroad to Russia. Four parallel lines of iron rails extended endlessly in each direction on the yellow gravel of the broad track—each fringed, as with a dirty shadow, with the dark strip burnt into the ground by steam and fumes." [17] *The Man without Qualities* opens as follows:

> There was a depression over the Atlantic. It was travelling eastwards, towards an area of high pressure over Russia, and still showed no tendency to move northwards around it. The isotherms and isotheres were fulfilling their functions. . . . In short, to use an expression that describes the facts pretty satisfactorily, even though it is somewhat old-fashioned: it was a fine August day in the year 1913.[18]

In the case of Kafka's and Mann's novels we have impersonal titles and personal openings; in the case of Musil's works, the opposite. Musil's titles indicate a crystallization of his thought around human qualities and problems, in spite of the paradoxical emphasis he seems to place in the works themselves on psychological and sociological events, and on impersonality in general. Here again we have an expression of the tension which seems to me to be basic to Musil's thought.

One is not surprised to find that a skeptical moralist in whose work ideas play such a central role should have a strong utopian orientation. This is centered in the mystic vision of a millennium in *The Man without Qualities* and is likewise implied, on a somewhat less exalted level, in the endings of *Törless* and "Tonka." Utopia was for Musil a dynamic rather than an absolute ideal, a direction rather than a goal. He observed in an early note for his major novel:

Writing is a doubling of reality. Those who write don't have the courage to declare themselves for utopian existences. They assume the existence of a country, Utopia, in which they would be where they belonged; they call it civilization, nation, etc. But a utopia is not a goal but a direction. However, all narrations pretend that it is something that has been or at present is, even if in some unreal place.[19]

But Musil's conception of utopia is nowhere very clear. He seemed to think in utopian terms as a compensation for the frustration and irrationality shown by mankind in its daily rounds. That Musil felt personally involved in this image of perfection is shown by the following diary entry, written early in 1940:

I lay no claim on success. But why not? I almost have it! The answer would certainly lead to the utopian aspect or the utopian assumptions of my work (in the individual works always occasionally!). To: literature as utopia. To the nonappetitive, contemplative man, for which much biographical material also speaks. The completion would have to be: determination of his function and task in the real world.[20]

The utopian direction of Musil's thought is closely connected with his concept of *werden*, of "becoming"; I shall return to this point shortly.

Against the background of these general characteristics of Musil's fiction some of the general qualities of his characters can be placed. The most salient of these qualities is the paradoxical nature of the characters: they are alive but pale, weak but impressive. While reading about them one has no very clear impression of what they are like; after closing the book one finds it hard to forget them. One feels in looking at Musil's characters as if a thin screen of translucent material had been drawn in front of the stage on which they act. Through this screen one can see their form and outline, but not their features. At the same time their thoughts and emotions are broadcast into the auditorium over loudspeakers. As fictional characters, then, these people lack vividness and focus, although at the same time one cannot deny that there is even in Musil's minor figures an opaqueness, an ambiguity such as one is conscious of in living people, which gives them an unexpected and attractive depth. The reason for this double impression is to be sought, I think, in the tension evident in Musil's thought between the theoretical and the personal indicated earlier.

Musil's characters also share a common basic problem, which may be stated as follows. Life has meaning only insofar as the individual finds for himself a place in relation to the society in which he lives. Before he can do this, however, he must find himself, and Musil focuses his attention on this latter process. The slice of time he deals with in all his works is a period of mental uncertainties and unsettling confrontations for his characters; habitual patterns of thought and action are dislocated and new ones must be thought out. The individual, in other words, has first of all a commitment toward himself; as soon as this is realized he can go on to become effective in the world. (Musil's basic criticism of the character of Arnheim in *The Man without Qualities* might be that he has become effective in the world without fulfilling this commitment.) Musil ends his works at this point. Törless, the "he" of "Tonka," Thomas, indeed all of his protagonists except Veronika and Ulrich—*The Man without Qualities* is unfinished—face by implication a more comprehensive and subtly better life at the end of their respective stories than they did at the beginning.

Musil's characters must painfully find for themselves the successive rungs in the ladder of identity which Joyce's Stephen Dedalus, in *A Portrait of the Artist as a Young Man*, noted in the flyleaf of his geography book: "Stephen Dedalus / Class of Elements / Clongowes Wood College / Sallins / County Kildare / Ireland / Europe / The World / The Universe."

Underlying this approach to fiction is the assumption that one cannot *be* something, but must *become* something. The verb *werden*, to become, is the hidden spring in Musil's works. It is not precisely the traditional concept of *werden*, a rather hazy tenet of faith in the dynamic process on the part of the early German Romantics; in Musil it is closely related to the term "possibility," as well as to a conception of utopia and the search for a new morality. Becoming implies change; possibilities can only be appreciated by a person who is aware of change; they can only be realized by a person who is capable of change. There is in each of Musil's works but one character who knows this, a doubter, a seeker, a "dreamer" in the sense in which Thomas uses the term in *The Visionaries*.

One can only become something in reference to a fixed standard; social values, for instance, must remain constant in order for an individual to change in reference to them. In his earlier writings Musil operated on this basic assumption. The school in *Törless*, the school and the official hierarchy in "The Completion of Love," even the feudal framework in "The Portuguese Lady" are expressions of this fixed order of the world. Indeed it is with this fixed pattern that the emotional fermentation of Musil's characters conflicts: they feel that they do not belong in it. But in *The Man without Qualities* Musil seems to have shifted his ground. Only after the First World War did he begin to work on this novel in earnest, and he was busy with it through a disastrous inflation and a second cataclysmic upheaval of traditional European values beginning with the rise of Hitler and culminating in the Second World War. In other words Musil fastened in his great novel upon a fixed social order *after its fall.* The result is a complete transformation into irony of the elaborate social structure of the Austro-Hungarian Empire which is the novel's framework —and also of Ulrich's search for his identity within this framework. The characters in this novel act as if the Emperor Franz Josef and the world he represents would survive the last judgment, to say nothing of the jubilee celebration planned for 1918 which plays such a large role in the first half of the book. Musil of course sharpened the irony by having the action of *The Man without Qualities* take place during the year from August 1913 to August 1914; if his intention had been otherwise 1890 or 1900 would have done just as well, since the decay of the Austrian Empire was not a recent phenomenon.

One effect of this in *The Man without Qualities*, as opposed to the effect of the stable frames of social reference in Musil's earlier works, is to give even greater weight to the theme of the individual, specifically to Ulrich's doubts about himself and his relation to the world. In an established order of things possibilities are irrelevant, and important, one might say, only to the rare individual who feels psychologically left out of this order. But in a disintegrating order possibilities become frighteningly real. Instead of automatically progressing from one well-marked station in life to another, the individual suddenly finds that he has to choose among many possibilities. The external falls away, the internal emerges with all its existential problems. In Musil's large second novel, it should be added, this is seen as a human problem and not a class question; Ulrich is a member of the aristocracy for whom all doors are open, and class consciousness is only passively present in the work.

Another prominent characteristic of Musil's personages is what might be termed a "common isolation." They react not to other people but to their own thought processes, and consequently are always either estranging or bewildering others. What does Törless know of the workings of Beineberg's mind, or Reiting's, or they of his? What does the "he" of "Tonka" know about the girl's motives for refusing to speak? What does Thomas know about Maria's thought, or Walter about Clarisse's?

This common isolation of Musil's personages is brought home by their sensory contact with the world, which leads not to physical action but to mental reaction, not to communication with others but to communication with self. In conversation they talk at rather than to each other. And, especially in *The Man without Qualities*, there is often a disconcerting lack of connection between a dialogue and an accompanying action which mirrors the lack of connection between mind and body, individual and environment.

The characters in Musil's works, consciously aware of the world through their sense perception of it, are by the same token made aware of their isolation from others. This same attitude is often expressed by Rilke, Musil's favorite poet, as for instance in the "Sonnet to Orpheus," I, 12: "Ohne unsern wahren Platz zu kennen, / handeln wir aus wirklichem Bezug. / Die Antennen fühlen die Antennen, / und die leere Ferne trug . . . / Reine Spannung." ("Without knowing our true place, / we act out of real relation. /

Antennas feel antennas, / and the empty distance bore . . . Pure tension.")

One might say that the basic *donnée* of Musil's characters is a sense of exclusion in an increasingly complicated and basically indifferent world. The infinite space that terrifies Musil by its silence is the vacuum between a person and his neighbor in a social context which makes the individual seem increasingly irrelevant. "We have won reality and lost dream," Ulrich exclaims at one point.[21] Musil's protagonists are all on the psychological defensive. They are conscious victims of their exclusion: Törless passes through a period of terror; Thomas loses his wife because of his detachment from life; Ulrich sees his life dissipate itself in "actions" which represent an increasing withdrawal from the world. All Musil's protagonists and most of his other characters could apply to themselves Rilke's lines: "Jede dumpfe Umkehr der Welt hat solche Enterbte, / denen das Frühere nicht und noch nicht das Nächste gehört" ("Every muffled turning of the world has such disinherited ones, / to whom neither the past, nor yet the future belongs").[22] But this exclusion is a mark of superiority as well as of frustration; the man apart in Musil's works is a marked man in both senses. Nor is there in Musil any of the sentimentality that Thomas Mann attaches to exclusion, as for instance in *Tonio Kröger*. More important, intelligent man in general, not the artist, is the outsider for Musil, and there is in his work no dialectical split between artist and bourgeois, or even—except in "Tonka"—between the upper and lower classes.

What seems to have interested Musil most in the problem of character was to establish some new method by which the individual could establish contact with himself and with other individuals. Basically he was seeking a new language to express in art the inner life of the emotions. Here he comes closest to an American writer who also began with psychology and was trying to do the same thing: Gertrude Stein. The most frequent process Musil uses in his fiction is not an association of words or ideas (the direction of Joyce) but, as has been indicated, an association of feelings (the direction of Stein). Ulrich's changing feelings toward the Prussian industrialist Arnheim, for instance, largely determine his attitude and behavior toward him; whatever Arnheim says or does is always colored in Ulrich's mind by a feeling of repulsion. Musil disengages, as it were, the emotional life which people lead beneath their "real" lives, and to which they generally pay no attention. This is largely what Gertrude Stein said she was attempting to do in her plays, to present not what happened but the *essence* of what happened, or what made what happened be what it was.

These general characteristics of Musil's work are put in perspective by his numerous sketches and projects; Musil's inexhaustible activity resulted not only in the few works he did write, but in plans for a great many others he did not. These last included among others such diverse items as a *Foundation of Literary Criticism*, an autobiographical novel *The Librarian*, a war novel in two parts *The Double Conversion*, *The Life of Vincent van Gogh*, and *The Development of Logic since Aristotle.*[23] It is interesting to conjecture why these far-flung plans were not carried out, a fact which takes on added significance because the works that Musil did write are all basically in a single vein.

But by far the most interesting of these projects is a plan for a satirical utopian novel which crops up in Musil's diaries several times between 1911 and 1920. This work was first to be called *The Land over the South Pole*, and later *The Planet Ed*. "Sketchiest program for it," Musil once noted, "a kind of satire on our spiritual relationships through representation of unlimited other possibilities." [24] Later he described it as a "moral experimental novel." [25] This plan, to judge by these short arresting descriptions, did not fall by the wayside exactly as the others did, for the "sketchiest program" describes with great accuracy—if from a more narrowly comic point of view—the subject of *The Man without Qualities*, which is also a "moral experimental novel" if ever there was one. Missing from Musil's second novel, however, is a *satirical* conception of utopia. While treated rather ironically, the utopia suggested in *The Man without Qualities* is of much too personal concern for both Musil and his characters to be handled with the degree of objectivity that satire demands. This might indeed be the reason for the deflection of *The Land over the South Pole* into *The Man without Qualities*, the social giving way to the individual as the center of interest.

The question of Musil's relation to past writers and to his contemporaries is extraordinarily difficult. His diaries reveal little of his opinion about other writers, and his works are with few exceptions—of which "Tonka" is the most important—more self-contained than derivative. But before examining Musil's relation to literary figures a brief indication is called for of a man who undoubtedly had a great impact on Musil, and with whose ideas, even when he was critical of them, Musil seems to have been in sympathy. This was the physicist, psychologist, and philosopher Ernst

Mach (1838–1916), on whom Musil wrote his doctoral dissertation in 1908.

According to Mach the only task of philosophy is the unification of the individual natural sciences. Completely rejecting metaphysics, he maintained that all knowledge is based on experience. Epistemologically Mach maintained that the individual is united to the external world only through sensory impressions. In the realm of pure physics Mach dealt both theoretically and experimentally with questions of physical and physiological acoustics, and he developed the method of stroboscopic investigation. He is also known for his investigations of the sensations of sound, space, and time.

For present purposes it is the affinity of Musil's and Mach's attitudes which are important, rather than Musil's technical and, significantly enough, largely negative criticism of Mach's specific ideas. This affinity operates, I would say, in four areas. These are Mach's concepts of (1) the complete relativism of physical and psychological phenomena, (2) life as a dynamic process of "becoming" (Mach applied the Darwinian theory of natural selection to mental as well as biological operations), (3) knowledge as based on experience, and (4) the need for a new synthesis of the natural sciences and philosophy, which corresponds roughly to the ideal expressed by Ulrich in *The Man without Qualities* of a fusion between "exactitude and soul."

Musil's dissertation begins with the significant statement:

> The times are past in which the image of the world in creation sprang from the head of the philosopher. Today philosophy seeks to formulate a new position for its relationship to that wide province of the discovered behavior of Nature according to laws; to that old longing for a proper comprehension of the

concept of matter and the concept of causality, and to the connections between physical and psychical, etc., including in this formulation all the methods and results of scientific research.[26]

One might say that Musil also envisioned his creative writing as a means to this end.

Illuminating for Musil's fiction too is the conclusion that Musil draws from Mach's emphasis on Darwinian natural selection, an emphasis which leads to natural selection of processes as well as of physical types; one might even go so far as to say that the way to Musil's utopia of "the other life" in *The Man without Qualities* is through a Darwinian selection of thoughts suited to man in a technologically oriented world. Both Mach and Musil are emphatic in rejecting causality, with its simplistic and absolutist overtones, as an outmoded concept. Both think rather in terms of "functional relationships," a more limited, flexible and scientifically appropriate approach—but one which, as indicated in the preceding chapter, conflicts with Musil's strong moralistic bent. Another source of conflict on this score is the principle of relativity which Musil deduces from Mach, calling it in his thesis the "skeptical interpretation" that "there is no real truth in a genuine sense, but only a practical, conservation-furthering convention."[27] Musil's fiction is also impregnated with a Machian emphasis on the interdependence of physical and psychical phenomena, and with Mach's contextual approach to both.

This brief discussion is meant only to indicate that in the development of Musil's thought Ernst Mach seems to have played an important part. What about his relation to literary figures of the past and of his own time? Here the scholarly "influence" game is to be especially avoided, since—the point can hardly be overemphasized—Musil's orientation was largely, and basically, nonliterary. This is not to say that his literary knowledge was at all deficient, even from an academician's point of view; indeed, in the "Considerations of a Slow Thinker" ("Bedenken eines Langsamen") of 1933 he mentions as the "grandfathers of today" Goethe, Nietzsche, Novalis, Hölderlin, Büchner, Keller, Stifter, Hebbel, D'Annunzio, Flaubert, Stendhal, Balzac, Dickens, Thackeray, Sterne, Swinburne, Verlaine, Baudelaire, Hamsun, Ibsen, Garborg, Jacobsen, Brandes, Dostoevsky, Tolstoy, and Gogol.[28] But Musil's literary education repeats the pattern of his life, that of "long choosing and beginning late." If we can believe Musil, looking back some thirty years to the time he was writing *Törless,* he had then read but little, and that imperfectly; he mentions Hauptmann, Hamsun, and D'Annunzio. He did, he says, know and love Dostoyevsky, although he does not claim to have understood him. Significantly he does not mention any of his Viennese contemporaries at this point.

Musil was one of the great cosmopolitans of art, and the writer who in his orientation toward life and in his conception of literary character stood closest to him came from another country. This was Stendhal, whom Musil admired and with whose life and work he was intimately acquainted. While the differences between them are great, the resemblances are striking: the same impatient ironic criticism of contemporary society; the same ironic detachment from life and scintillating wit; the same areas of interest in literature, the social and the erotic; the same penchant for systematization and schematization; and the same naïve faith in future fame and contempt for contemporary neglect. It is also worth noting that Musil's Ulrich has some of Julien Sorel in him; his career in the army had been the result of a desire to emulate Napoleon, but he lost interest in the military when, after rising to the rank of lieutenant, he was called down for trying to seduce a relation of an influential financier.

Musil's process of assimilating what he read seems to have been unusual, and for this reason one must be careful in linking him to other writers. Musil rarely discusses writers or their works in his diaries, but merely refers to them as something known. His stepdaughter claims that he read little fiction, but that his wife read omnivorously—a book a day.[29] It would seem reasonable to infer from this that some literary osmosis took place between the couple.

One might also infer from both Musil's diaries and *The Man without Qualities* that, following his natural bent for the essayistic and the epigrammatic, he dipped into other writers' works more than he studied them consistently. When Musil does mention a writer in his diaries it is usually to comment on some striking personal quality or idiosyncrasy; often the writer is merely mentioned by name as an example of some general quality, as when Musil speaks of the "example of Stendhal, who read the Napoleonic Code before working." [30] Musil seems to explain this curious process of assimilation in speaking of how the "gifted young man" acquires culture:

> He finds what "speaks" to him, here Stendhal, there Euripides, then a contemporary, etc. From each only this or that effect. He proceeds without a system, and yet in such a way as if he were allowing himself to be led by the system of his being. (He allows himself to be led by his gift, by his talent.) (N.B. The extremely unsystematic element in my own development.)[31]

Musil's attitude toward his contemporaries was distinguished by the same qualities. Here too one has the impression that, although he was familiar with their work, they did not touch him closely. In notes for an autobiography Musil noted how little aware he was of contemporary literature when he began to write:

The relation of the writer to his time. That one does not go along; remains behind, misses the connection, doesn't contribute, etc. I began specifically literarily: Dostoyevsky, Flaubert, Hamsun, D'Annunzio, and others: not one contemporary was among them! They all wrote from twenty to a hundred years earlier![32]

Hofmannsthal is mentioned twenty times in Musil's diaries, notebooks, essays and speeches, but never discussed. Typically, Musil's approach to other writers is through the process of generalization, as in this 1936 diary entry: "It often takes an entire lifetime to come to a right conclusion about a person. How often have I changed my judgment of Rilke, of Hofmannsthal. Favorite conclusion from this: that there is no objective judgment, but only a 'living' one."[33] The student of Musil does not know what these judgments were.

Musil's personal reaction to his literary contemporaries, as with literary figures of the past, is scarcely to be gleaned from his diaries. In the case of Freud, Musil's passing comments again show a thorough acquaintance, but the only extensive reference to him is a paragraph in "From a Rapial and Other Aphorisms" ("Aus einem Rapial und andere Aphorismen") under the heading, "The wish is father of the thought!" Here Musil asserts:

The development of psychological attitudes which has taken place in the last fifty years and more can well be characterized as a deposing of reason and understanding in their significance for the spiritual life (human life) through emotion (*Affekt*). Freud has accomplished most of this, yet he commands only a stretch in the line of development that begins before him and will end after him.[34]

Here again, as usual, Musil shows a very acute perception of the stature of his contemporaries from a detached point of view. This often caused him to be disgusted with popular taste. He wryly notes, for instance, "I left Vienna in 1931 because red and black both agreed that in Wildgans they had lost a great Austrian writer." [35] Karl Kraus, the most satirical and polemical of Viennese critics, was one of Musil's particular bogeymen. Musil wrote in 1930 or 1931 that "there are two things against which one can't fight because they are too long, too fat, and have neither head nor foot: Karl Kraus and psychoanalysis." [36]

The foregoing discussion has indicated, if only tangentially, some of the central problems and attitudes upon which Musil's fiction is based, and some of the characteristics of his art. Since Musil lived for his writing, these problems and attitudes can best be examined more deeply by discussions of his individual works.

III

The Confusions of Young Törless (1906)

MUSIL'S first novel is the only one of his works in which there are children, and in this novel Musil chose the child as his subject matter, the adolescent child. Adolescence is the point in the development of the individual at which the direction of the mind becomes of critical importance, and it is the point in the development of the individual at which suffering and the feeling of helplessness are likely to be most intense. The conjunction of these two elements, the domains respectively of psychology and art, best explains why a young psychologist with literary ambitions chose adolescence as the sphere of his first book.

One does not have to be a Freudian to appreciate the pain and confusion of the adolescent's groping to find himself. Without the protection of mature experience, the factor which enables the adult to order his picture of the world, the child is more open to shock and pain. The adolescent is beginning to be consciously aware of violent feelings within himself, feelings which he does not see reflected in the adult world or in the attitude of others. This often leads him to be more cruel than the adult because he is intensely concerned with himself and has not yet learned to be considerate of others. It leads him to be more cruel than the adult also because, suffering himself, he often seeks to make other people suffer. The adolescent can inflict pain and confusion on others too by imitating adult ideas and attitudes without understanding them. Where can these qualities of adolescence be observed better than in a boys' boarding school, where by constant contact adolescents can exercise enormous power over each other without either restraint or understanding from the adult world? Musil worked all of these elements into *The Confusions of Young Törless*, and it is the novel's great merit that Musil makes the reader see and feel the inner struggles of a boy changing from child to adult.

Törless is the son of well-to-do parents who is sent to an upper-class boarding school in the eastern part of the Austrian Empire. After a brief friendship with a young prince he falls under the influence of two older classmates, Beineberg and Reiting. These discover that a third classmate, Basini, has pilfered money from other students. Using this knowledge as a weapon, they force the soft Basini to become their creature, and make him an object of their sadistic intrigues and weird philosophizing. Törless is a semiactive observer of all this; he develops and then grows out of a homosexual attraction to Basini, and rejects Beineberg and Reiting, for whose ideas he has never had any sympathy. When the scandal breaks over his three classmates, Törless tries to explain to the school authorities his mental fascination with the others. The school authorities do not understand him. Törless feels that a chapter in his development is closed and leaves the school, ready to grow up. For Törless, the discovery that others also have deep inner struggles, and can be cruel and violent, is new. Coming as he does from a well-ordered and enlightened home, he is overwhelmed by this discovery, which causes in him the "confusions" of the title.

From this brief description one might expect a certain type of novel, stormy, tragic, passionate. In reality it is quite different, and the difference lies in the author's attitude toward his subject. For Musil, Törless the boy and the experiences he goes through are object and examples. This is not the story of the suffering of an individual, but an examination of the psychology of an adolescent and, perhaps even more, an examination of the psychology of an adolescent representing a general type of human psychology at a particular stage of development.

The story of what happens to Törless and the significance of what happens to him are presented in the book in two distinct ways. The story is presented by a reporting of conversations and by minute description of externals reminiscent of the naturalism of the 1890's; the significance of the story is presented by following from a detached point of view—essentially that of an adult psychologist—the changes of states of feeling in the boy's mind. Musil's attempt to express these states of feeling by using a literary vocabulary, as opposed to a clinical one, gives rise to the basic literary device in *The Confusions of Young Törless*, a device which might be called the "tensed image." I think "tensed" is the right word here for two reasons: the images attempt to convey to the reader's *intellect* an impression of Törless' *feelings*, and the language itself, as in English metaphysical poetry, is stretched almost to the limits of what language can do.

Let me give two examples of this kind of image. In describing Törless' thoughts and feelings, which are from the beginning the sole focus of attention in the novel, Musil tells us that while writing letters to his parents Törless felt a peculiar sensation: "Like an island full of wonderful suns and colors something rose up in him out of that sea of gray sensations which pressed around him coldly and indifferently day after day."[1] And spending his days thinking of the letters he will write home at night, Törless feels "as if he is carrying, hidden on an invisible chain, a golden key with which he will open the door of miraculous gardens when no one is looking."[2] "Island" and "key" are words which have many levels of association intellectually as well as emotionally. The same is true for "colors," which is linked to "island," and "gardens," which is linked to "key." The terms of Musil's figures of speech are almost always concrete, as in this instance, and they are also spun out with some complexity. One responds emotionally to the image, but one also has often to work out the ways in which the terms of the image are connected with each other. This technique is found in all Musil's works, but especially in his earlier ones; its high-water mark occurs in *The Temptation of the Silent Veronika.*

Why did Musil develop and use this type of imagery? The answer, I think, first becomes clear in *Unions,* where this technique is much refined and expanded. This answer would be that Musil is trying to convey through language mental processes which, partaking simultaneously of conscious and subconscious states of mind, produce a blurred continuum of thought and nonverbal feeling. The tension in the images arises from the violence with which nonverbal or subverbal feelings are yoked together with a highly intellectual complexity.

The tensed images in *The Confusions of Young Törless* indicate not so much the loneliness as the secretiveness of Törless' thoughts, while his body—almost, one has the impression, in another world—is mechanically going through the motions of his school environment. Indeed this relationship between the foreground of psychology and the background of environment is maintained throughout the book, and is the most important reason why this novel cannot be regarded as an indictment of the old-style continental military boarding school.

These images are one way in which Musil develops the general significance of Törless' feelings; another is the prominence of ex-cathedra statements by the author. The reader is seldom left to deduce the significance of a process in the novel; he is told what it is. Typical is the statement near the beginning summing up Törless' homesickness: "He thought it was homesickness, longing for his parents. But in reality it was something much less distinct and more composite." [3] Here, before the actual story has begun, when the protagonist has barely been introduced to the reader and his individuality is as yet unestablished, the author is already leaving him in favor of a broader point of view. In enlarging on this statement Musil even intrudes personally into the novel:

> For the "object of this longing," the image of his parents, was really no longer contained in [Törless' feeling]. I mean this certain plastic memory of a beloved person, corporeal as well as remembered, which speaks to all the senses and is preserved in all the senses, so that one can do nothing without feeling the other person, silent and invisible, at one's side.[4]

This early tendency in Musil shows that the principle of "essayism," so important in *The Man without Qualities*, is already present in embryo; indeed near the end of his first novel, in a passage about thought which interrupts the action of Törless' flight from the school, we have a full-fledged example of it. One might conclude from this generalizing tendency that it was for Musil not so much a matter of literary technique as of the way he thought.

But this tendency to generalization in *The Confusions of Young Törless* makes the reader see Törless in a wider perspective than would simple narration. By constantly turning from the specific to the general it broadens the experiences of a single individual into a study of certain attitudes of the state of adolescence. Combined with another, less obtrusive factor it reduces the impact of Törless' suffering. This factor is indicated by a key phrase which changes the entire perspective of the novel and greatly increases the distance not only between the protagonist and the author but also between the protagonist and the reader. "Törless could *at that time* . . . ,"[5] Musil writes, and this term occurs repeatedly throughout the work. This factor is the perspective of time. The present action of the novel is seen not as the continuous complete time of action, but as a point in time. Törless is even described at some length as an adult. By means of this device Musil is rather obtrusively stepping back from his subject and makes the reader do likewise. The description of Törless in later life makes his present suffering and confusion seem less immediate.

In view of this tendency to generalization and temporal removal it is not surprising that as an individual Törless remains shadowy. What little characterization he has had as he first appears is given either directly by the author or through a verbalization of the boy's thought. Nor do we know what Törless looks like, except for indirect indications: a minor figure, the prostitute Božena, notes at one point that Basini is about as tall as Törless, and in an impersonal description of Basini we are told that he was somewhat bigger than Törless. But the other important characters, Beineberg, Reiting, Basini, and the mathematics professor, are all physically described, either impersonally by the author or as seen through the eyes of the other characters (usually Törless'). Törless thus remains shadowy against a background of characters who are sharper than he is. We are given none of those details of appearance or characteristic action which provide a seed crystal around which the reader's impressions of a character may crystallize. Beineberg's gawkiness, overrefined hands, and obtruding ears or Basini's softness of body and effeminate features are examples of such seed crystals. It is true that the reader knows a good deal about Törless' *mental* qualities if he puts together the bits and pieces of information which are scattered throughout the novel. Thus the reader knows that Törless' leading quality is a well-developed imagination, that his mind is superior to Beineberg's or Reiting's, that he suffers from an overactive sensitivity, that he is a dutiful son, and that his thinking is morally sound from a conventional point of view. But the reader's picture of Törless is incomplete. The point is important because what is true of Törless in this respect is also true of almost all the major characters in Musil's works, especially of Ulrich in *The Man without Qualities.*

This peculiar relation of the main character of the novel to the other figures is chiefly responsible for two effects, both of which indicate that Musil's procedure in characterizing Törless was deliberate. These are the impression of dissociation of Törless from the other characters (although present at their sadistic intrigues he stands very much apart from them) and the impression of dissociation from the background (at the end of the book Törless leaves without regret the school to which he has never felt any sense of belonging).

Why does Musil so emphasize this dissociation of Törless? Because, I think, Törless' major problem is not one of social adjustment but of mental confusion; and in this confusion he is very much alone. He has a recurrent sense of the unreality of people and things. He is always aware that people and things have two faces, the ordinary aspect of everyday and a large, dark, unfathomable, and horrible essence. This awareness tortures him. Törless is pursued by these thoughts in looking at the blue sky, or thinking of imaginary numbers in mathematics, or trying to puzzle out what Basini means to him. This confusion finds expression in Törless' sudden flight from the school and in his "confession" before the investigating board, to which he says:

> No, I wasn't wrong when I spoke of a second, secret unnoticed life in things! I—I don't mean it literally—it's not these things that are alive, it wasn't Basini who had two faces—but there was a second face in me, which looked at everything with eyes not of reason. The way I feel that a thought comes to life in me is the way I feel too that there is something alive in me when I look at things, when thoughts are silent. There is something dark in me, beneath all thoughts, that I can't measure with thoughts, a life that can't be expressed in words and yet is still my life.[6]

Törless' dissociation from his schoolfellows and from the school is of course not complete. They are his two frames of reference, by which he takes a stand in relation to the world.

It is true that the authority of the school, to which—in

the figure of the mathematics professor—Törless once turns for help in connection with his concern about irrational numbers, responds only with a puzzled impatience. But at least this indicates that Törless turns to the adult world of the school for help when he needs help. Even if this world does not understand him, it represents to him an anchor of sanity. The impression is given that it is regrettable but not tragic that the professor does not understand Törless' excitement about irrational numbers, or that his parents, when he writes them a letter about Basini, send back a reasonable enlightened answer which is no help to Törless. Clearly these adults do not appreciate the terror for the boy of his situation, or the immediate threat to himself which Törless feels. It is remarkable that, misunderstood by the adult world to which he appeals, Törless does not throw himself wholeheartedly in with the depravities of Reiting and Beineberg, but rather falls back upon himself. Unlike Thomas in *The Visionaries* and Ulrich in *The Man without Qualities*, Törless manages to preserve in the midst of the difficult situations in which he is placed an essentially untouched sense of his own individuality. This sense, it must be added, is apparently much clearer to Törless than it is to the reader—the result of one of the risks an author runs in trying to present the mind of a character without presenting the character.

One of the merits of this short novel, which suggests so much more than it says, is that its depth extends beyond its protagonist. The figures of Beineberg, Reiting, Basini, and the mathematics professor are bafflingly complex. The professor, for instance, the least important of these four, has an aura of unstated complexity which is quite unusual for a tangential character in a novel—an aura which will be seen again in minor characters in Musil's later works, such as Josef in *The Visionaries* and Diotima in *The Man without Qualities*. For example, while Musil speaks approvingly of the young teacher's contribution to mathematics, there is more than an overtone of satire in the presentation of his sloppy person and shabby rooms. Törless is repelled by these externals: "He could hardly hope any longer that this man was in possession of any significant knowledge, since it was clear that not the slightest sign of it was evident either in his person or in his entire surroundings." [7] And at the end of the novel, when the board of school officials is trying to decide what to do with Törless, the professor again reveals an insensitivity to human feeling when he says of Törless: "He was really so strange that I almost think he has a disposition to hysteria." [8]

Beineberg has inherited his father's warped mysticism, which he warps even more. This mysticism affords Musil the occasion for the sharpest satire in the novel. Beineberg is one of those ambiguous people whose attitude toward the world, indeed toward life, is hostile. These characters see the world through a murky veil of undigested ideas by whose light they are always right and the rest of mankind always wrong, and their only conception of being related to others is to acquire power and exercise it ruthlessly. This can be seen not only in Beineberg's arguments with Törless and in his use of Basini, but also in his attitude toward his fellow plotter Reiting. Beineberg wants to use Reiting's depravity as a tool to get even with him, or perhaps to assert his power over him, and this, together with other obscure motives, is part of the complex motivation which determines Beineberg's attitude toward Basini.

We are told little about Reiting, but Musil manages to

suggest a great deal about his behavior. Reiting is an admirer of Napoleon who finds great pleasure in conducting malicious intrigues. He has a gift for setting people against each other, for organizing mob action. He loves power for its own sake; he does not, like Beineberg, seek to rationalize the desire for power by appealing to some supposed metaphysical justification. This difference between the two boys might account in part for the current of hostility between them which is subtly indicated by Musil.

Musil's interest lies in Törless, and not in Beineberg and Reiting; hence he does not develop these latent conflicts, or indeed the characters themselves to any great extent. But he indicates enough about them to cast unwittingly, from 1906, a long, dark, anticipatory shadow forward to the rise of Nazism. It would be an overstatement to say that there is a political element in *The Confusions of Young Törless.* But the unscrupulous drive for power of Beineberg and Reiting must be considered an embryonic political problem, and as such points the way to the political problems which form an underlying but important part of Musil's other novel, *The Man without Qualities.*

In the case of Beineberg and Reiting there is just one important reservation to be made: their attitude toward Törless seems to be artificial. Their complete acceptance of this boy who holds himself back from them is never satisfactorily explained. When toward the end of the novel Törless makes Basini reveal the entire affair to the school authorities, it seems somewhat contrived that the active suspicions of the evil pair should never fall on Törless. Not only was Törless the only other person who knew what had been going on, but also the other two had noticed how close to Basini Törless had become. This might be explained in part by the essential isolation of the individual characters from each other, for each person sees things only from his own perspective. Thus Reiting sees Basini as an object on which he can vaunt his power, while Beineberg sees in him a chance to test his peculiar mystical theories and Törless sees in him the embodiment of the strange double nature of things. None of the figures sees the perspective of another: Törless, for instance, is completely uninterested in Reiting's intrigues and is irritated by Beineberg's woolly thoughts.

Basini is, for Törless, by far the most important of these three characters. The action of the novel is conducted by Beineberg and Reiting with Basini as its object; Törless is the mind, the consciousness, through which this action is reflected. But he is also drawn into the action; during a holiday in which he and Basini are among the few people who stay behind at the school all of his ambivalent feelings toward Basini come to the surface. The image of Basini in Törless' mind becomes associated more and more with sexuality. At the same time Basini gradually loses, both for Törless and the reader, his individuality; he is seen from an increasingly distant viewpoint, more and more as an object. Musil makes plain that it is not Basini but something he represents which exercises on Törless such a powerful fascination. It is not merely Basini's ambivalent sexuality (although this is the form in which it expresses itself) which so upsets Törless as it is Törless' frantic awareness of the "two faces" of things, an awareness which he tries to express in words in his "confession." Musil keeps this latter perspective uppermost, so that when Basini becomes Törless' creature, and then his leader, and when Törless suddenly and completely loses interest in him, the reader is made aware that this dramatic climax is not the point of the book.

The point of this novel is a different and far more complicated one, of which Basini is but one aspect. Törless is preoccupied by Basini, but he seems to be more emotionally upset by the problem of irrational numbers in mathematics. For Törless the problem is that irrational numbers are imaginary; they are negative quantities, they do not exist. But by means of these negative quantities a positive system of thought is constructed. One starts with real numbers and one ends with real numbers in a higher order, but in between lies the negative. This becomes for Törless an emotional problem. In reckoning with imaginary numbers, he says:

There are at the beginning quite solid numbers, which can represent meters or weights or anything else that is concrete, and which are at least real numbers. At the end of the reckoning are similar things. But both of these hang together through something that doesn't exist. Isn't it like a bridge of which only the two piers are there, and which one yet strides over as confidently as if the bridge were all there? For me such a reckoning has in it something that makes me dizzy; as if it were a piece of a road to God knows where. But what is really uncanny for me is the power which is contained in such a reckoning, and which holds one so fast that one still lands on solid ground.[9]

This problem was to haunt Musil through *The Visionaries* and become perhaps the keystone of his conception of *The Man without Qualities.*

It is made quite clear in *The Confusions of Young Törless* that this problem is not incidental. It comes up repeatedly, and is made to seem as important to Törless as his complex of feelings about Basini; indeed in his mind Basini seems to become an example of the problem of the two faces of things, the real everyday one and the hidden power behind, of which the central expression is in real and irrational numbers. When this problem becomes too much for him, Törless suddenly runs away from the school. He is found two days later in a neighboring town and brought back, and it is after this that he makes his statement to the school authorities. Although his sudden flight is not explained, but simply presented, it is not too difficult to understand. It is the flight of someone from circumstances and problems which have become too much for him.

Törless is the first but far from the last of Musil's characters to take sudden flight. Regine in *The Visionaries* and Ulrich and Agathe in *The Man without Qualities* also flee in the same way, and in the physical separation which is an important element in Musil's minor works, as for instance in "Claudine," "The Temptation of the Silent Veronika," and "Grigia," there is something of this same quality of flight. At least in Musil's three major works the flights follow the same pattern: a period of great mental tension brings on a deep depression in which the character realizes the basic irrationality of human behavior and the contradiction between this irrationality and the pretense of rationality which enables man to endure life. Then, either before the flight or after, comes a flash of attempted explanation. Thus in *The Man without Qualities* Ulrich passionately presents his idea for a "World Secretariat of Exactitude and Soul" to Count Leinsdorf, and in *The Confusions of Young Törless* Törless struggles to formulate before the school officials his feeling about the two faces in things. Both pleas—for this is essentially what they are—fall on deaf ears.

This failure of communication is not due simply to insensitivity on the part of those to whom these pleas are addressed. We can see in Musil's first novel that this failure has a deeper, one might almost say necessary, cause in Törless himself. This cause is his inability to articulate feelings (that is, the irrational) as thoughts (the rational). In other words, what Musil as author can attempt to do, verbalize what are essentially nonverbal processes, his character himself cannot do. But by the time Törless struggles to express this feeling articulately at the end of the novel Musil has clearly indicated to the reader in the course of the work what kind of struggle it is; a very solid background for Törless' inarticulateness has been built up, a perspective against which it can be understood. This background consists of Musil's use of tensed images and impressions combined with actions to explore throughout the novel the twilight world between the levels of thought and feeling. This would explain why Musil chose as epigraph for his first novel a quotation from Maeterlinck:

"In some strange way we devalue things as soon as we give utterance to them. We believe we have dived to the uttermost depths of the abyss, and yet when we return to the surface the drop of water on our pallid fingertips no longer resembles the sea from which it came. We think we have discovered a hoard of wonderful treasure-trove, yet when we emerge again into the light of day we see that all that we have brought back with us is false stones and chips of glass. But for all this, the treasure goes on glimmering in the darkness, unchanged."[10]

In a curious way in this novel the characters, situation, and action demand a much larger scope than Musil gives them. Where, for instance, others would see evil and depravity in the actions of Beineberg and Reiting (they are fitting precursors to their soul mates in Gide's *The Counterfeiters*), Musil does not. He uses these figures for his purposes, and when they have fulfilled their function they disappear like stones in a pond. Although Musil sets the stage for a tragedy in the manner of Hesse's *Under the Wheel,* he does not write one. Musil is interested in probing, not in dramatics; dramatic conflicts in his works are incidental. His real interest lies in the playing out of the given behavior of different individuals in the same context, and from this he derives a commentary on human action in general. *The Confusions of Young Törless,* Musil's first novel, points the way through the intervening works to his second, *The Man without Qualities.*

IV

Unions (1911)

THESE two stories—called "novellas" (*Novellen*) on the cover of the first edition and "two tales" (*zwei Erzählungen*) on the title page [1]—present two attitudes toward love between the sexes, the yea-saying and the nay-saying. These works might best be characterized as attitude studies rather than character studies. The heroine of the first story is a sensualist with nymphomaniac tendencies who glories in her feelings, while the heroine of the second is a psychotic ignorant woman who expresses her strong sensual love in unnatural ways and finds a negative pleasure, as well as frustration, in withholding it from natural completion. Both heroines are examples of that *Ausnahmemoral*, or morality of exception (fundamentally a behavioristic concept), which so fascinated Musil in his observation of life.

The first story, "The Completion of Love," has an atmosphere of warmth and tenderness not found elsewhere in Musil. The atmosphere of the second story, "The Temptation of the Silent Veronika," is one of frustration. The two tales thus complement each other, the more so in that they have a common base of erotic, sexual love. But eroticism and sex are not presented for their own sake in *Unions*—it is hard to imagine these stories hiding behind a suggestive cover on a drugstore bookrack—but for what they represent; Musil's treatment of sex is closer to that of a manual of abnormal psychology than to the school of Henry Miller. The adultery that is the incident of the first story actually bestows a final perfection upon the marriage it "disturbs"; the refusal to love in the second story leads to near suicide and waste of individual potentialities. The basic assumption of both stories is that fulfillment of the potentiality of the individual is desirable, however unconventional such fulfillment might prove to be. The heroines of these stories are for all practical purposes the only characters in them; and one never loses the feeling in reading *Unions* that in spite of Musil's impressionistic technique these women tend more toward being clinical case studies than individuals with problems. This feeling seems to derive in part from the author's detachment from his heroines; in both stories observation is a much more important element than identification.

This detachment vitiates the two stories in that it makes the characters, for all the psychological subtlety with which they are presented, singularly colorless. To appreciate this one need only compare Musil's Claudine and Veronika with the heroine of a similar and nearly contemporary story by Gertrude Stein, "Melanctha" in *Three Lives* (1908). Musil's detachment from his heroines also seems to be responsible for the reader's impression that as a whole these works are considerably less impressive than the individual scenes and observations of which they are composed. Still, while *Unions* might be obscure to the reader from a rational point of view, he finds himself responding emotionally with some degree of empathy. This is especially true of "The Temptation of the Silent Veronika." The impressionistic technique which is responsible for this effect deserves closer attention, especially since after pushing it to the breaking point in "Veronika" Musil abandoned it almost entirely in his later writing.

Musil's impressionistic technique becomes somewhat clearer if we think of impressionistic technique in painting and of what "impressionism" in general is. In this connection some of the observations made by Richard Hamann in his book *Der Impressionismus in Leben und Kunst* (*Impressionism in Life and Art*) are illuminating.[2] Speaking of impressionist painting Hamann notes that it is concerned with individual figures rather than groups (one notes the extreme concentration in Musil's stories on the heroines). He further observes that impressionist painting avoids large connecting color surfaces, concentrating rather on building up each surface from innumerable little spots and points of different tones. This latter process is also the one that Musil has used in *Unions*, and when thought of in these terms the stories become more comprehensible. In a philosophical discussion of impressionism which draws heavily, significantly enough, on Mach and the philosopher Heinrich Rickert, Hamann says that in impressionism psychological states (*Seelenzustände*) have become the real object of fiction (*Dichtung*). And when Hamann summarizes the basic characteristics of impressionism he almost seems to be talking about *Unions*. These major characteristics are: thinking and speaking in images, exaggeration, the animation of thought, and, instead of a systematic unity, a "monism of gradual transitions" which recalls Musil's theory of literature as "the path of the smallest steps." A critical examination of these two stories will help to give a clearer idea of an important phase of Musil's art.

"The Completion of Love"

According to Musil's stepdaughter this was Musil's favorite work, and the only one of his works which he reread.[3] The action of the story can be quickly sketched. The heroine, Claudine, leaves her husband to visit a small town where her daughter by one of a number of earlier illicit love affairs is at school. On the train she meets a bearded stranger; several days later she allows him to seduce her. But if ever in literature action was incidental, or rather accidental, it is in "The Completion of Love."

The story opens in the middle of a dialogue between husband and wife. The first sentence, a question, sets up the story: "You really can't come along?" Claudine asks her husband.[4] The husband's replies show a certain irritation. A note of intimacy and looming separation, as in the later story "Grigia," is immediately struck in this conversation. For some time the speakers are referred to only as "the man" and "the woman." The first few pages establish their complete mental union; they follow each other's unspoken thoughts and feelings perfectly. But the husband's irritation and their agreement that "every brain is something lonely" [5] indicate a subterranean tension.

The man remains undeveloped in the story; from the second page Musil's images focus exclusively on the woman. As the story proceeds, one feels that Claudine's latent hostility toward her husband is a defensive means of preserving her own identity—an element we shall see later in Maria in *The Visionaries* and in Agathe in *The Man without Qualities.*

In a Rilkean passage the couple thinks of a "third," of

many thirds who form a counter to their Adam-and-Eve relationship. Their conversation is highly stylized and borders on the metaphysical; the images are almost exclusively of erotic sensuality, for instance: "Then one of them said, and it was as if one lightly stroked a violin. . . ."[6]

Musil uses imagery involving ordinary objects in Claudine's environment, such as a clock, or snow, to communicate to the reader not her feelings and thoughts themselves but her impressions of them. The reader is thus presented with a nebulous impressionism that is apparently meant to correspond to the half-conscious half-unconscious continuum which occupies the mind during its waking hours; or, to put it more precisely, Musil here seems to be operating on a level *between* the conscious and the unconscious. Rather than using free association, or showing the content of thought in the mind of his protagonist, Musil is here presenting instead the subjective impressions which they create in that mind as they well up into the area of semiconsciousness.

Musil's thought-impressionism—I do not think that "stream of consciousness" is the right term for this process—is much less direct than similar techniques used by Joyce and Woolf, and considerably less directed; Claudine is not going to any lighthouse, much less returning to the earth-mother after an Odyssean quest. Where Joyce and Woolf use the stream-of-consciousness technique as a means to an end, Musil's technique is both means and end. This would explain the importance of the story line in Joyce and Woolf and its unimportance in "The Completion of Love." In this respect Musil is somewhat closer to his compatriot Schnitzler, except that the latter uses the technique in a much more formal and straightforward manner, usually presenting as taking place in the minds of his characters a relatively logical association of conscious ideas. But Musil is here closest of all to Gertrude Stein and to her idea of presenting essence rather than substance. One might say that Musil encounters the same basic difficulty as Joyce, Woolf, and Stein in that he is trying to verbalize what are essentially nonverbal processes—which may be regarded as an attempt to overcome one of the basic limitations of literature as an art. The interesting term "stream of *consciousness*" is itself an indication of this difficulty, since what is really meant by it is a stream of semi- or subconsciousness. The following passage from "The Completion of Love" is an example of what Musil is trying to do here:

Und während sie ihr Herz schlagen fühlte, als trüge sie ein Tier in der Brust,—verstört, irgendwoher in sie verflogen,—hob sich seltsam ihr Leib in seinem stillen Schwanken und schloss sich wie eine grosse, fremde, nickende Blume darum, durch die plötzlich der in unsichtbare Weiten gespannte Rausch einer geheimnisvollen Vereinigung schaudert, und sie hörte leise das ferne Herz des Geliebten wandern, unstet, ruhelos, heimatlos in die Stille klingend wie ein Ton einer über Grenzen verwehten, fremdher wie Sternlicht flackernden Musik, von der unheimlichen Einsamkeit dieses sie suchenden Gleichklangs wie von einer ungeheuren Verschlingung ergriffen, weit über alles Wohnland der Seelen hinaus.

("And while she felt her heart beating, as if she bore a beast in her breast—disturbed, fled somewhere within her—her body rose strangely in its silent oscillation and closed itself around it like a large, strange, nodding flower, through which, suddenly, the ecstasy of a secret union, stretched into invisible distances, shudders; and she heard softly the distant heart of her beloved wander, sounding fluttering, restless, homeless in the silence like a note of music blown over borders, flickering strange like starlight, a note seized as by a monstrous maze by the uncanny loneliness of the consonance which was seeking her, sounding far beyond all that land where souls are at home.") [7]

This kind of erotic imagistic impressionism builds up for pages on end, giving the reader an excellent impression of the waves of feeling that sweep over Claudine; as psychological characterization it is extremely effective. Musil's ability to give a convincing impression of the thought processes of nonintellectual or even ignorant women, such as Claudine and Veronika, is one of his most striking gifts. There are in every one of his works women of one or the other stamp, from the prostitute Božena in *The Confusions of Young Törless* to Bonadea and even Diotima in *The Man without Qualities.*

In its erotic imagistic impressionism *Unions* might also be compared with one of the most ambitious attempts to convey passion through music, Wagner's *Tristan and Isolde.*

Musil might have used as a motto for both these stories Novalis' phrase "the mysterious pathway leads within," for nowhere else in his works is the physical world so shadowy. There is no physical description at all of Claudine or her husband and only the most fleeting description of the other characters. Externals, such as the description of the room in which the conversation between Claudine and her husband takes place, are systematically subordinated to internal states of feeling and through imagery made to reflect these internal states. Indeed the external world is so dependent on the internal in this story—as opposed to *The Confusions of Young Törless,* where the external world exists as a separate, objective reality—that at one point the school town and its houses change as Claudine's feelings change. The real processes of both stories in *Unions* go on in the minds of the heroines, as Musil indicates when he speaks, in reference to Claudine, of "the great context of feeling of her existence, braided through the years." [8] It is, in other words, the web of feeling rather than action which constitutes for Musil in these stories the important plane of human activity. The enormous slowing-down of both time and action in order to concentrate on the subtle shadings of feeling—one again thinks of *Tristan and Isolde*—is what Musil referred to in connection with *Unions* as "the maximally laden path, the path of the smallest steps." [9]

Claudine takes the train alone to go see her daughter. Separated from her husband for the first time, she feels herself psychologically and erotically vulnerable, and finds herself sinking into her emotional past, which had been effectively forgotten in her complete devotion to her husband. Claudine does not regret this past, which time has dimmed: "Nothing remained of it but the memory of a strange cloud of feelings, which had confused and aroused her for a while like a cloak suddenly thrown over her head, and which had then swiftly slid to the floor." [10] Although in her earlier life she had yielded repeatedly to her nymphomaniac tendencies—her daughter had been the result of a momentary fascination with an American dentist—Claudine, who prefigures in this respect the nymphomaniac Bonadea in *The Man without Qualities*, had never lost the belief "that everything she did did not basically touch her, and essentially had nothing to do with her." [11] Like Törless, she is conscious of a deep inner life paralleling, but not connected with, her outer daily life.

The body of the story establishes not Claudine's individuality but her isolation, the isolation which seems to be in Musil's works the prime mark of the *condition humaine*. Claudine lives in a silent world of feelings which is mirrored in the muffling snow, a very prominent element in the story. Speech rarely intrudes into this world, and when it does it usually breaks her mood. Her isolation appears the more marked when compared with the harmony of her relationship with her husband at the beginning of the story, where speech is seen merely as an extension of inner silence.

It is, then, against a background of separation, isolation and eroticism that the incident of "The Completion of Love," the seduction of Claudine, occurs, and it occurs as a complete and almost comical accident. The bearded stranger, a *Ministerialrat* (a government official), first comes to her attention on the train; the rest of the story, approximately the second half, is concerned with the slow crystallization of her feeling around this "third" who comes between her and her husband. It is a crystallization in the specifically Stendhalian sense of the term, and one feels that the author of *On Love* would have been enchanted by "The Completion of Love." It must, however, be emphasized that the *Ministerialrat* is as accidental an object for Claudine's feeling as Basini was for Törless', and this accidentality here provides Musil with an occasion for some of his sharpest irony. The man preens himself on his ability as an irresistible lady-killer, unaware of the ridiculous picture he presents to Claudine and to the reader, who sees him through Claudine's eyes.

The *Ministerialrat* is the ironical element in "The Completion of Love"; Claudine's relationship with her husband is treated with tender seriousness. It is perhaps not accidental that the vehicle of the irony in this story is one of Musil's most successful characterizations; the man is perfectly sketched in his few banal remarks and equally banal actions. In his opening gambit to Claudine on the train he compares the landscape ("an idyll, an enchanted island" [12]) to a beautiful woman. Claudine's reaction to this remark sets the tone for her subsequent attitude toward him: " 'How silly,' thought Claudine, but she did not find the right answer immediately." In this first interchange the attitudes of both are established, and the rest of the story is elaboration.

The *Ministerialrat* obviously prides himself that it is his elegant technique which, after several days of hesitation on her part, conquers Claudine. She, however, is no Emma Bovary, and yields to him for reasons which have nothing to do with him at all but well up from her past emotions. The most urgent of these reasons seem to be her basic sense of insecurity and an outburst of suppressed resentment and hostility against her husband; when the man asks her if she loves her husband, Claudine replies "trembling and decidedly": "No, no, I don't love him at all." [13] In this total failure of mental contact between the lady and her seducer Musil is again demonstrating how his characters operate on different levels without breaking through to each other. The dominant impression even of Claudine's intimate relationship with her husband is that neither of them understood the other as well as they thought. This failure of contact becomes at times grotesquely comic: "Then the Ministerialrat kissed her: 'So you love me?' And Claudine still found the strength to object: 'No, I love being with you, the fact, the accident, that I'm with you. One could be sitting with the Eskimos. In sealskin pants. And have hanging breasts. And find that pretty.' " [14]

On a more serious level, Claudine's submission seems to be

a way of proving her own identity vis-à-vis her husband, whom she loves. Sexual union with this stranger, contrasting with the intercourse she has had with her husband early in the story, is for her a token of reunion with her husband, an overcoming, in some obscure sense, of her hostility. And as a result of this experience, which takes place in "a small town cut off from reality,"[15] Claudine understands her love for her husband. The final sentence of "The Completion of Love" is: "And very far away, as children say of God that He is great, she had an idea of her love."[16]

"*The Temptation of the Silent Veronika*"

An earlier version of this story, "The Enchanted House" ("Das verzauberte Haus"), is a traditional, almost banal tale of seduction. The transformation into the shimmering abstract impressionism of "The Temptation of the Silent Veronika" is startling. Even upon repeated readings one cannot say precisely what *happens* in the finished version. And yet as an impression of a situation seen chiefly through the eyes of an ignorant, mentally disturbed woman, much as the first part of Faulkner's *The Sound and the Fury* is seen from the point of view of the idiot deaf-mute Benjy, this story is effective, although in the last analysis its effectiveness seems limited.

Veronika, who foreshadows Clarisse in *The Man without Qualities*, has committed sodomy with a dog, and has—perhaps—had intercourse with Johannes, who is, as far as one can gather, a relative of some sort (he belongs to the same family and lives in the same house). She also has apparently unfulfilled sexual urges toward Demeter, a third member of the family and household. A man with the name of the Greek goddess of the fruits of the earth Demeter is, as one might expect, rude, vital, and earthy. (In the earlier version Demeter, a soldier, is the leading male character and far more prosaic.) Veronika refuses three times to marry Johannes, a weak, sensitive character who is frustrated by her withdrawal from him. She sends him off to commit suicide, but once he is gone from the strange house Johannes sensibly refuses to oblige. Veronika is left in the house with Demeter to become a frustrated sexless creature like her aged spinster aunt.

Veronika's ruling passion appears to be a fear of sterility. This is expressed in her frank conversations with Johannes about his lack of virility and Demeter's apparent abundance of it. Veronika compares their house to "a world in which we are alone, a sad world in which everything becomes crooked and strange as if under water" [17]—which is very much the way this world looks to the reader. Veronika's isolation, of the most extreme sort, is behind the solid wall of her psychosis; like Claudine, but in a negative rather than a positive way, she lives largely in a world of remembered feelings rather than present actions. In a specific description of a kind quite rare in Musil's works Veronika is described from Johannes' point of view; the essence of this description is an impression of wild, almost animal sensuality.

One curious feature of this story is the conversation. It is not at all realistic, but rather as if one person's feelings were speaking directly with those of another in exaggerated verbalized pictures without passing through the "censor" of the superego.[18] Characteristic is the remark that Veronika makes to Johannes: "You are sometimes as impersonal and withdrawn as a candle in the dark, which is nothing itself and only makes the darkness larger and more visible." [19] This kind of conversation is not to be found in *The Confusions of Young Törless* nor, except at the beginning, in "The Completion of Love." In both these latter works characters' states of feeling are presented imagistically, but conversation between characters is of the everyday variety. The conversation in "The Temptation of the Silent Veronika" is also at the opposite extreme from that in *The Man without Qualities,* in which both id and ego are burned away and conversation involves only the superego. This difference reflects Musil's different orientation in the two works; in the early story he is interested in presenting an example of irrational behavior, while in the later novel the background of such behavior is a much more important element.

"The Temptation of the Silent Veronika" has certain affinities of mood and language with Rilke's *The Notebooks of Malte Laurids Brigge,* which appeared in 1910, a year before *Unions.* Rilke succeeds better than Musil in presenting a decaying neurotic household, perhaps because of the pervasive sense of morbid autobiographical introspection in *Malte* which is totally absent from Musil's work. Musil, in trying to use lyric language clinically, and maintaining through his technique a detached objectivity, succeeds here only in being opaque. In this respect "The Temptation of the Silent Veronika" differs also from the morbid rural visions of the Austrian poet Georg Trakl (1887–1914): although the garment Musil wears in his story was put on for the occasion, as its sophisticated imagery and somewhat clinical handling show, the same is not true of Rilke and Trakl, whose methods were an organic part of their subjects and of themselves.

In "The Temptation of the Silent Veronika" Musil carries the impressionistic technique of "The Completion of Love" one step farther along his "maximally laden path," and one step too far. All one can see in this story are individual spots of color; the spots do not combine, as they do in the first story, into the impression of a form. It is significant that in his subsequent works Musil abandoned this kind of impressionism; in the later stories "Grigia" and "The Portuguese Lady," for instance, the characters are much more clearly defined while the *setting* is used as the base of impressionistic evocation.

But whatever its merits compared with other works, "The Temptation of the Silent Veronika" remains an interesting experiment on Musil's part to see how far he could carry his attempt to express feelings through words. And taken as a whole, *Unions* is one of the most interesting experiments in modern fiction.

V

The Visionaries (1921)

AFTER the dust has settled around *The Man without Qualities*, Musil's only serious play, *The Visionaries*, may one day be considered his finest work. It contains in distilled form, and with the greater strength of a distillation, most of the important elements of the later novel as well as many of its subordinate concerns. It is true that *The Visionaries* lacks the broad perspectives of *The Man without Qualities*. Unlike the novel the play does not present a society on the brink of dissolution; but it might be argued that Musil's talent was better suited to the smaller scope of this drama which presents a household on the brink of dissolution. Both works have as their central concern Musil's statement of the dilemma of the modern man of intellect, the man who has tamed nature through reason's child, science, only to realize that when it comes to human relationships reason and science are not enough. Furthermore, although the setting and dialogue of *The Visionaries* are nonrealistic, the play's characters are more convincing, even on reading, than are those in any other of Musil's works. Partly as a result of this, Musil here comes closer than he does anywhere else to directly involving the reader in his cogent but peculiar statement of the emptiness of modern life.

A word should perhaps be said about the differences between Musil's dramatic characterization and that in his prose works. The most striking of these is his heavy reliance in *The Visionaries* on physical appearance and physiognomy as a primary means of indicating the basic nature of his characters. Very rarely in his prose writings, and then in an unemphatic way, does Musil describe his figures. Another significant distinction is the way in which, in the play, the characters bring out each other's qualities in every situation. There are parallels to this in Musil's prose—some of the scenes between Beineberg and Törless, for example—but they are neither numerous nor sustained.

The Visionaries was published in 1921. (It was not performed until 1929, and although Musil objected violently to the production of this truncated version the play itself had some success.[1]) It is a serious sophisticated play with a comic element; Musil labeled it simply *Schauspiel* ("play"). It would appear at first glance to belong in the company of Molière's *The Misanthrope* and Hofmannsthal's *The Difficult One* (*Der Schwierige*), but it differs from such works in at least two fundamental respects: it is concerned with thought rather than social convention (although bourgeois social attitudes are satirized in the character of Josef), and hence cannot be described as a "comedy of manners," and the play's unsettling actions and implications have the effect of removing it completely from the domain of comedy.

The relationships in Musil's play serve only to delineate the psychological and metaphysical postures of the individual characters; the dialogue is rather on the level of thought process than of social relations, somewhat in the manner of T. S. Eliot's *The Cocktail Party*. The people in *The Visionaries* hardly engage in conversation in the usual sense, but speak their own attitudes. Consequently the dialogue is atomistic as well as partially abstract, and this reinforces the isolation of the individual figures in a context of minimal physical action. *The Visionaries* displays what might be called a Racinian existentialism in the intensely painful isolation of its protagonists, whose frequent and hard collisions with each other produce—or reveal—only frustration. Relief of sorts in this savage mental struggle is provided by the stock-comic "virtuous" character of Regine's companion Fräulein Mertens, a student who is described in the cast of characters as "*cand. phil.*," with a "good-natured face, reminiscent of a schoolbag, and with a seat which has become broad from listening in the halls of wisdom," [2] and by the seriocomic detective Stader, to whom are given some of the basic philosophical statements of the play.

The fundamental affinities of *The Visionaries* thus seem to be more with a play like Joyce's *Exiles* (1918) than with the so-called comedy of manners. A brief comparison with *Exiles* might throw some light on Musil's play, although there can be no question, I think, of any direct connection between the two works. Joyce's play also involves a triad of people no longer young who have been friends from childhood; Bertha in Joyce's play has much the same quality as Maria in Musil's, and Beatrice similarly resembles Regine. The permissiveness of Joyce's hero, Richard Rowan, in the winning over of his wife by his friend Robert Hand, has much in common with the permissiveness under similar circumstances of Musil's hero Thomas.

But the similarities between the two works should not be overemphasized; there are differences, too. *Exiles* lacks the intellectual intensity, emotional charge, tragic overtones, and complex plot structure of *The Visionaries*. Also, Richard

Rowan is too detached from things, his story too muted, to bear extensive comparison with Thomas. It is also significant that the political overtones of Joyce's play are completely absent from Musil's. Then too, there is in Musil's work a remarkable note of personal urgency. The body of *The Visionaries* was written, in rough form at least, between February 1911 and March 1912.[3] It is, I think, especially illuminating that many of Musil's most personal observations about himself and his world occur in his diaries during this period, concurrent with notes on and about the play. It seems to have been for Musil, who was then in his early thirties, a time of unusually intense self-examination.

The plot of *The Visionaries* can be briefly summarized. Josef is Regine's incompatible second husband. Her first, Johannes, had some years before committed suicide in the suburban house of her brother-in-law Thomas, a successful professor and famous scientist. The action of the play takes place in this house. Anselm, an unstable and neurotic former professor, has insinuated himself with Regine and convinced her and her companion, Fräulein Mertens, to flee to Thomas'. Once there, Anselm drops Regine, and in an atmosphere of what amounts to complete permissiveness transfers his attentions to Thomas' large wife Maria (who is in some ways similar to Joyce's Molly Bloom). All the major characters, including Anselm, have been friends since childhood. By employing a detective to dig up that part of Anselm's past which they, his ostensible friends, did not know, Josef and Thomas expose Anselm for the liar, coward, and cheat that he is and send him away. Although shocked by the revelation, Maria decides to follow him anyway. (It should be emphasized that Anselm, who is already married, is no conventional seducer; he has a pathological need of controlling people that seems to be asexual.) The pattern of the relationship between Maria, Thomas, and Anselm repeats that of Claudine, her husband, and the *Ministerialrat* in "The Completion of Love"—a close attachment of long standing built on a sand foundation of irritation, in which the arrival of a "third" upsets the original relationship between the couple. The "third" himself is more or less accidental; the fruit was in any case ripe for the plucking. But while in the earlier story the final result of this displacement is a rapprochement between the original couple, Maria and Thomas in *The Visionaries* act like a double star pulled apart by the near approach of a third star to their gravitational field; one member of the pair goes spinning off through space while the other is disturbed in its orbit, or, it may be, destroyed by collision with the intruder.

The main action of the play involves Anselm's attempts to convince Maria to leave with him, and Thomas' inability to prevent it. A subordinate action concerns Regine's hatred for her husband, her gradual "recovery" from her infatuation with Anselm, and as she slowly loses her grip on reality her attraction to Thomas, whose cerebral nature she to some extent shares. In the play's final scene Regine—and in a lesser way Thomas—finding themselves unable to cope with the realities of Josef and Anselm, regress to memories of their childhood in much the same manner as do Frédéric Moreau and his friend Deslauriers at the end of Flaubert's *Sentimental Education*. A minor but significant point in the play is that all four marriages (Regine's two, Thomas', and Anselm's) are childless. This contributes to the isolation of the characters; by way of contrast Archie, the son of Richard Rowan and Bertha in *Exiles,* forms a link between his father and mother.

Significantly, all the characters in *The Visionaries* have counterparts in *The Man without Qualities.* There are many areas of identity between Thomas and Ulrich, Regine and Agathe (and Clarisse), Maria and Diotima, Anselm and Arnheim, Josef and Agathe's husband, even between Stader and General Stumm von Bordwehr.

The world of *The Visionaries* is singularly hermetic. The action of the play consists mostly of a series of sharp verbal battles which take place in three rooms of a peculiarly unreal house in a period of eighteen hours. Of the eight characters the five important ones are with the exception of Anselm related to each other by blood or marriage; as has been mentioned, they have all been friends since childhood (even Stader had once been a valet in the household of Regine's and Maria's family). Except for Stader and Fräulein Mertens, all seem to belong to the upper middle class or lower aristocracy. Most of the characters are about the same age ("between 28 and 35," Musil notes in the stage directions; "only Fräulein Mertens is perhaps a little older, and Josef is past 50"[4]). As far as their ages and stations in life are concerned, then, they are fairly homogeneous.

This excludes an action built on external conflict, for instance a discrepancy in age or social position, and leaves as the only possible battleground the minds of the participants. In making the ages and stations of his major figures roughly alike Musil perhaps also meant to suggest that their respective personalities might be considered as one personality split up into its components, or perhaps to indicate that in modern society the "whole man" can no longer exist. Thomas, the scientist, is cerebral and completely rational; Maria is sensuous and physical; the more complicated Regine is a frustrated happiness-seeker chasing the will-o'-the-wisps of her childhood, while Anselm combines all the attributes of irrationality and Josef all those of bourgeois conventionality.

The focus on abstracted mental process in *The Visionaries* is further reinforced by the play's tangibly metaphysical atmosphere, for the setting is partially abstract. The stage directions for the first act, which warn the reader of the metaphysical nature of what is to come, are worth quoting:

> The scene represents a dressing room, which is connected to the adjoining bedroom by a large closed folding door. Entrance door on the opposite side. Large window. Ground floor. View of a park.
>
> This scene must in its execution represent imagination as much as reality. The walls are of linen; doors and windows are cut out in them, their openings painted; they are not fixed, but restless and movable within narrow limits. The floor is fantastically colored. The furniture recalls abstractions like the wire models of crystals; it must be real and usable, but as if it had originated through that process of crystallization which at times arrests for a moment the flow of impressions and separates out the individual impression in abrupt isolation. Above, the entire space fades into the summer sky, in which clouds are swimming. It is early forenoon.[5]

The result of these hermetic proceedings and isolating abstractions is a rigorous exposure of human psychology and motivation, but nothing more. There is no "moral" to be drawn from the play because morality is not the standard by which things are judged in it. (The attempts of Josef to interpret the actions of the other characters moralistically only show his narrowness of outlook.) As in his other works Musil is here working with behavioristic rather than moral standards. Nor is there any "point" to the play in the sense of a neat message; its lesson lies rather in the unfolding process of action and reaction among the protagonists. In this sense it is rather similar to the process of "chemical reaction" in Goethe's novel *Elective Affinities*. Musil's characters do not change or develop, but unfold; and, except that its figures are made to face up to themselves more honestly than they had done before, *The Visionaries* hardly conforms to Musil's description of art as "a partial solution of what ought to be." [6] The play's feeling of futility seems to be deeply connected with this unfolding process, which denies the possibility of change. It almost seems as if Musil were here exploring the implications of Goethe's line, "Geprägte Form, die lebend sich entwickelt"—"stamped form, which unfolds itself in living."

Each of the main figures in the play has his eyes opened about his own nature, and realizes—usually with a feeling of helplessness—that his actions proceed from that nature. Maria realizes that she has been leading what for her is the wrong kind of life with Thomas; Anselm proves himself to himself again; Regine decides to sacrifice herself by returning to her husband because she realizes that she has been too self-indulgent in the past, and Thomas finds yawning beneath his feet a Pascalian abyss which has been waiting for him for years. Of them all, however, it is Anselm and Regine who by their activity and ambiguity dominate the play. While Thomas is more interesting than either Anselm or Regine, and is the character with whom the reader feels the greatest identification and sympathy, he is too much the passive victim of forces that he can neither understand nor effectively oppose. Maria, on the other hand, is not fully presented.

But the resolution of these problems can hardly be considered permanent. There is no reason to think that Anselm will be any happier with Maria than he was with Regine or his own wife (for him the important thing seems to be conquest rather than possession); Regine can hardly be thought of as maintaining her self-sacrifice, or her sanity, for several decades as Josef's wife. Rather the problems of these people are isolated from the flux of life and time, exposed to a pitiless analytical searchlight, and then dropped back again into the cosmic flow.

Musil uses physical appearance as his first means of characterization in this play. Before the play begins, the reader has a distinct impression of Maria's soft sensuality (she is "tall, dark, heavy; the movements of her body are like a melody played very slowly"), Thomas' cerebral character (he is "almost small, thin, and sinewy only as is a beast of prey; correspondingly his face, under a magnificently strong forehead, almost escapes notice), Anselm's ambiguous sensuality ("the sensual part of his face is fascinating"), Regine's complexity ("dark, indeterminable; boy, woman, dream-illusion object, malicious magic bird"), and an indication that Stader is meant to be more than a simple comic figure ("Stader was once a handsome youth, and is now a capable man").[7] Upon this base and that of the semiabstract setting, the first act sets up the figures and their interrelationships while the second and third present an acting out of the situation. It should be emphasized that the density of characterization in *The Visionaries* is so great, and the interrelationships of the characters so subtle, that any critical discussion can only hope to hint at the actual complexity of the play.

This is so much the case that one wonders whether an audience which saw the play only once could really grasp all of its many facets. Thus the following discussion of the three major protagonists and Stader is in no sense to be regarded as exhaustive. Although they will be examined separately, Thomas, Regine, and Anselm cannot be completely isolated. But by considering the complex that surrounds each of them I think one may obtain a clearer view of the play and also of the double center around which it revolves—Anselm, the psychic hurricane's eye, the pivot of storms and lightnings, and Thomas, the center of gravity of the play's entire system of values.

Thomas moves from an illusion of strength to a realization of weakness. The contrast is extreme between the confident and successful man who playfully pokes his head in at the door at the beginning of the play to joke with Regine, and the helpless man broken by despair at the final curtain as Regine takes leave of him. Here is material for a tragedy, and in a sense this is one, or would be if the action of the play had been set within a moral framework and if Thomas had actively brought about his own downfall. But one feels that here as elsewhere (notably in *The Confusions of Young Törless* and *The Man without Qualities*) Musil seems especially anxious to avoid the tragic implications of his material. After exhausting the resources of reason in exposing Anselm, Thomas can only look on helplessly while Anselm conquers his wife. Woven into Thomas' permissiveness is an essentially fatalistic conception of life. He feels that since the attraction of Anselm and Maria to each other grows out of their own natures, nothing, in the absence of an external force such as social convention, can prevent their coming together. (Again compare Goethe's *Elective Affinities.*)

Thomas, the rationalist who sees too many sides to things and too many possibilities in life, suffers the fate of another of Musil's men without qualities, that of Ulrich in *The Man without Qualities:* paralysis of the will through overdevelopment of the intellect. Like Ulrich, Thomas might be called top-heavy; and his loss of Maria, who prefers the inconstant warmth of Anselm to her husband's cold self-sufficiency, is a kind of punishment for this disproportion. Musil seems to have felt the limitations of his scientist hero Thomas in much the same way that Swift felt the limitations of his rational Houyhnhnms, that in the last analysis a life based exclusively on reason is somehow insufficient. After Thomas has at one point accused Anselm of being a failure, Anselm retorts: "Absolute ruler of a paper kingdom!" [8] And it is a salient feature of *The Visionaries* that everything the characters say to each other in the course of the play is true.

An image which Thomas uses in his first significant speech strikes the keynote of the relationships in this play: isolation. "One pulls one's own skin like a dark hood with a few eye- and ear-holes more and more firmly over one's head," he says. "It is *we* who could now be brother and sister, Regine," he continues, establishing a common bond between them.[9] Thomas recalls the visionary plans for a "new man" —suggestive of expressionist programs—which he, together with Johannes and Anselm, had drawn up years before. The key to this plan had been a "possibility of creation" (*Erschaffungsmöglichkeit*); [10] the fatal Musilian term "possibility" again comes to the fore. The conversation between Thomas and Regine turns to Anselm; they characterize him before he appears. Regine, whom Anselm has recently victimized, admits calmly to Thomas that everything Anselm does is some sort of spiritual deceit.[11] It appears from this conversation that Anselm's problem is a pathological desire to overcome the limitation of his isolation; he wants to attach other people to himself in a desperate attempt to prove his worth.

Thomas is upset by intimations that his old and close friend Anselm might have dishonest motives. Maria enters the argument, and we learn that Anselm has been an unsuccessful professor and is a general failure. The attitudes of the three toward him are unsettled; none of them quite knows what to make of him, although Regine tells Fräulein Mertens that Anselm has designs on Maria. Thomas does not see this until Josef presents documentary proof gathered by the detective Stader. When Anselm refuses to come and talk to him, Thomas becomes bitterly angry. Making common cause with Josef (who had previously threatened him professionally for sheltering Regine), he exposes Anselm to the entire company. In laying Stader's evidence before Maria and Regine, they expose Anselm's false *actions*—a procedure based on an appeal to reason. Maria (Thomas is fighting for her as Josef is fighting for Regine) is convinced that the rational arguments are true, but maintains that they are not important; Anselm's feelings, and her feeling for him, have a higher value.

This appeal from reason to intuitive feminine sympathy defeats Thomas, whose outlook begins and ends with the resources of the rationalist. He becomes aware of his own deficiency but realizes his inability to overcome it. He sees what it is that drives Maria to Anselm, and in the third act is finally completely reduced by it. Maria asks Thomas what he would do if she went away with Anselm. Thomas, no longer angered but resigned, gives an answer that will recur again—the same answer that Richard Rowan gives in a similar situation in *Exiles:* "I don't know. Go." Maria, struggling with tears, replies: "Yes, that's the way you are. Renounce everything, if a new plan looks better to you. I know that you like me. You know that I'll never forgive Anselm. Never! But even this poor human being gives off more calm and warmth than you. You want too much. You want everything to be different. That may all be all right. But I'm afraid of you!" [12] Thomas finally *tells* Maria to leave: "Go, Maria, you must," and, after hesitating, she runs out of the room as Thomas starts toward her.[13] At this point Stader comes in to throw Thomas' brilliant scientific success in his teeth with the comic suggestion that Thomas become a partner in the firm of Newton, Galileo, and Stader. It is here that the word "visionaries" occurs for the only time in the play, and with many ironic overtones: "Yes, even I was a visionary!" Stader tells Thomas. "But I've come to the conclusion that that isn't enough." [14]

Thomas, then, is resigned to his wife's departure, but his bitterness finds another outlet. He remarks to Josef that he has come to the realization that "love for a selected person is really nothing more than repulsion against everyone." Josef misunderstands the remark, saying: "You're without feeling." Thomas counters this and goes on, like Musil in *The Confusions of Young Törless* and "The Completion of Love," to emphasize the importance of love as a force and the accidentalness of its object.[15] Then, in the play's most violent outburst, Thomas turns on Josef, castigating him as a paragon of bourgeois values.[16] Slightly deflecting his wrath, Thomas also bitterly contrasts the technological advances of science, with which he as a scientist has been directly involved, with their promise of a new humanity that never comes. The scientist, his personal life undermined by forces of irrationality with which he cannot deal, sees his professional accomplishments—the product of the rationality of which he had been so proud—also crumble.

Thomas then withdraws into the despair of an empty, satirical view of life. His companion in the play's final scene is Regine, who seems to be in the first stages of mental breakdown (representing withdrawal from a reality which has become too much for her). Thomas refuses to help her. She asks him many times during this scene: "What shall we do now?" On one occasion Thomas replies: "Nothing, Regine. Gilded nuts never hang on real trees. One only looks for them there, which is remarkable enough." [17] From disillusioned bitterness Thomas sinks to a sense of the unreality of life. In answer to Regine's question about how people fill life up he says: "They cheat, of course. They have a profession, a goal, a character, acquaintances, manners, designs, clothes. Alternative assurances against being swallowed up in the million-mile deeps of space." [18] At this point Pascal turned to God; but where can a modern scientific rationalist turn? Thomas looks into a mirror, as it were, and sees nothing but his own face.

There is, however, a faintly positive side to this disaster. Goethe says in his *Maxims and Reflections* that "the acting man is always without conscience; no one has conscience but the observing man," [19] and Thomas might be said to have changed from the acting man into the observing man. This would explain the muted indication of redemption in Thomas' final speech. For it should not be forgotten that in Musil's scale of values the observing man, although often victimized, occupies a superior position in relation to the acting man. One thinks of Törless in relation to Beineberg, and Ulrich in relation to Arnheim.

Thomas' final dialogue with Regine becomes a kind of monologue with two voices. Its sense it that life goes on, that the individual is only a representative of the species (Darwin's "struggle of life" is referred to specifically by Thomas in an argument with Josef [20]). This dialogue assumes something of the character of the chorus in Greek tragedy; one feels that Thomas and Regine are commenting on the action of the play rather than speaking as participants—victims—in that action.

For the last time Regine pleads with Thomas to do something. Thomas replies that there is nothing to be done, that man is alone. This view of the bankruptcy of life is not quite absolute, as has been indicated above, although the positive note struck by Thomas is quite feeble in the face of the play's overwhelming sense of futility. This "creative condition" to which Thomas refers seems to be a self-conscious detachment of the individual from his environment. But surely such a detachment can only be potentially creative, for the artist must synthesize as well as observe. Detachment, while perhaps a necessary precondition of both observation and creation, is but a small part of creativity. It does not even imply creativity as a necessary consequence, and this, it seems to me, is the weakness underlying Thomas' speech which is called forth by Regine's accusation that he is "a man of reason without feeling":

> No no, Regine, if anyone is a dreamer, it's me. And you're a dreamer. Those are apparently the people without feeling. They roam around and watch what those other people do who feel themselves at home in the world. And bear something in themselves that these other people don't feel. A sinking at every moment down through everything into the bottomless. Without perishing. The creative condition.[21]

Musil wrote in his diary on August 31, 1911 (the surrounding entries, from May to September of that year, are full of the problems of *The Visionaries*):

> Vienna—Florianigasse 3. You roam around among these people, to whom you belong in spite of everything, and who are strange to you. You see how they amuse themselves, what they're doing; they have erected statues. Your opposition is not merely this general basic mood out of which we also otherwise act, but it is a detailed opposition tied by many fine filaments to life itself.[22]

Ulrich, in *The Man without Qualities,* contains much of his author's intellect and biography; Thomas embodies more of his author's feelings than does any other of Musil's characters.

Thomas, Maria, and Anselm form one group in the play; another, in many respects as important, is formed by Thomas, Josef, Anselm, and Regine. Regine is caught in a web formed by these three men and her dead first husband, whose memory she reveres. She detests Josef, pities and forgives Anselm, and is attracted to her brother-in-law Thomas by a partial affinity of character. (Regine's attraction to Thomas foreshadows in many respects both that between Ulrich and Agathe and that between Ulrich and Clarisse in *The Man without Qualities.*) In Regine the tension between the tyranny of reason and the primacy of inner feeling—which Thomas represents more clearly on the one hand and Maria more clearly on the other—is so great as to result in mental dissociation. The dichotomy between inner life and outer actions, already seen in both Törless and Claudine, reaches in Regine its semifinal stage; only the insanity of Clarisse lies beyond. In the first act Regine tells Stader:

Listen, "Ferdinand": A person can be as holy inside as the horses of the sun god, and outwardly he's what you have in your files. That's a secret that your [detective] institute will never uncover. One does something, and inwardly it means something quite different from what it means outwardly. But in time one has only done that inwardly which has happened outwardly. One no longer has the strength to transform it! [23]

As the play opens, Regine is talking with Fräulein Mertens. Immediately an unobtrusive term is used which is repeated so often that it assumes in the course of the action a special significance. This is the word *wirklich:* "So you're *really* not superstitious?" Regine asks her companion.[24] Throughout the play Regine is tortured by the nature of the real and of reality, a preoccupation she shares with *The Visionaries*' other cerebral character, Thomas. At the end of the first act she screams at Anselm: "You beast! Anselm! We are nothing real! Whether we lie or not, are good or throw ourselves away: something is meant with us that we can't ever explain. You knew that, and have given away all our realness (*Wirkliches*)." [25] Maria and Anselm, who are more spontaneous, do not consider reality an abstract problem, while Regine and Thomas are tortured by the polarity of something "real," even though they have only a hazy notion of what it is, and by the illusion they feel their lives to be.

Like Thomas, Regine too is touched by the fatal consciousness of possibility that is at once the curse and the blessing of all Musil's cerebral characters. Early in the play she remarks to Fräulein Mertens, just as Thomas enters:

Every human being comes into the world with powers for the most unheard of experiences. Laws don't bind him. But then life always lets him choose between two possibilities, and he always feels: there's one missing, always one, the undiscovered third possibility. And one does everything one wants, and has never done what one has wanted. Finally one loses all capability (*Schliesslich wird man talentlos*).[26]

In another argument with Fräulein Mertens, Regine scores one of the play's major points: "Love is never love! A physical meeting of fantasies, that's what it is! A fantastication (*Phantastischwerden*) of [*as her eyes, seeking a comparison, gaze around*] chairs . . . curtains . . . trees . . . with a person as the center!" [27] This, it should be noted, is the central point of Stendhal's *On Love*, a work that throws light on character relationships in all Musil's writings. This attitude in *The Visionaries* is important because it releases Regine, Maria, and Thomas from the conventional literary bond of "married love," a release emphasized by Josef's stubborn adherence to the conventional attitude. The detachment implied by Regine's dissociation of the emotion of love from its object is shared by Thomas; this detachment is part of the necessary preparation for removing Anselm's abduction of Maria from the realm of melodramatic adventure.

Regine's denial of love might in part be due to the conflict in her mind between her dead husband Johannes, for whose suicide she has deep feelings of guilt, and her insensitive second husband. This conflict, which is precipitated by Josef's arrival to reclaim her at the house in which Johannes died, leads to a minor nervous breakdown. Josef, a sterling representative of middle-class values, describes Regine as she appears in that scale of values: unsensual, objective, reasonable, cool. (Judging people by their external actions rather than by their internal attitudes, presenting as it does a different perspective, might be regarded as a positive function of Josef in the play.) Josef obviously has no intimation of Regine's inner life, and this is undoubtedly one of the things for which she hates him. Josef thinks of Anselm as a neurotic seducer and demands that he be punished; until Anselm is exposed before the entire company, he does not see that Maria rather than his wife is now the object of Anselm's desires, and that Regine has recovered from her infatuation with Anselm.

Regine is also the only person in the group who comes to Anselm's defense when Thomas and Josef, armed with Stader's files, are pressing their attack on him: "Don't fall in with their reason!" she shouts at him. "They want to trap the invisible creature in you!" [28] That Regine can say this about the man who has brought out her latent weakness is another indication that Anselm is far from being a conventional villain, a point that can hardly be stressed enough.

Regine eventually rids herself entirely of her infatuation for Anselm, and can finally say: "Now I stand in the clear, and everything is extinguished. Today I have become a reasonable person." [29] From this point on she moves much closer to Thomas. But it is made quite clear that she has lost something by this decision. Anselm is for her above all an external symbol of irrationality. Once this symbol is lost, the strong irrationality of her own inner being begins to make itself felt, and she turns to Thomas as a defense against being swallowed up by it completely. There is a feeling of both submission and frustration in Regine's decision to sacrifice herself by returning to Josef; certainly her tenuous hold on sanity cannot long survive this move. The only person she can accept and be accepted by on her own terms, then, is

Thomas, and in the final act she and her brother-in-law form a spiritual union. At one point in this "diamonologue" Regine expresses a basic malaise that is shared by all Musil's detached protagonists: "There is something in us that is not at home among these people; do we know what it is?" [30] She pleads with Thomas to do something, only to be met with the answer that there is nothing to be done. They kiss each other with a kiss of desperation, which Fräulein Mertens, happening in at that moment, misunderstands and uses as an excuse for leaving. Thomas and Regine are now the only people left in the house. After Thomas has made his final confession of bankruptcy, Regine kisses him and quickly leaves. The play ends as Thomas calls after her: "But Regine! . . . No, no, she won't do anything rash [*but still he stands up and goes after her*]." [31]

"There are problematic natures," Goethe wrote in *Maxims and Reflections*, "who are not up to any situation in which they find themselves, and whom no situation satisfies. From this arises the monstrous conflict that consumes life without enjoyment." [32] Such a person is Anselm, the most problematic figure in *The Visionaries*. The other characters are fascinated by this man who is literally, in Musil's terms, a man of possibility; while Thomas *sees* the many possibilities of life, Anselm *is* them. Among the other protagonists only Regine shares to some extent Anselm's profound ambiguity. In the first act Thomas says to Anselm,

[*as if he wanted to force Anselm to recognize himself*]: There are people who will always only know what could be, while others, like detectives, know what is. Who hide something flexible where the others are firm. An intimation of being able to be different. An undirected feeling without inclination or disinclination between the elevations and habits of the world.

A homesickness, but without home. It makes everything possible!

Maria protests: "But that's just going to turn into theories again!" Anselm himself replies: "Yes, those are theories. You've found the right word. But how horrible it is if theories mix in with life and death." [33]

The body of the action of the play involves attempts by the other figures to explain the character of Anselm. The total effect of these expressions is prismatic; the others see Anselm from their own individual perspectives and in their own individual terms. This again reinforces the strong feeling of personal isolation which runs through the play. Josef's description of Anselm as sick, for instance, is descriptively true but beside the point. It is the judgment of Antonio about Tasso in Goethe's play *Torquato Tasso*, or the judgment of the Reverend Mr. Morell in Shaw's *Candida* about Marchbanks (who has much in common with Anselm). Regine perhaps understands Anselm best. It is she who explains how Anselm can be both genuine and false at the same time, in a statement that also does much to explain the character of Arnheim in *The Man without Qualities*. She says to Thomas, "[*in an outbreak of despair*]: Haven't you ever heard someone sing falsely with genuine feeling? Why shouldn't someone feel genuinely with false feelings?!" [34] This defense of Anselm by Regine together with the ambiguous attitudes toward him of his other "victims" Maria and Thomas indicates that Musil did not intend the spectator or reader to condemn Anselm.

Anselm's gradual winning-over of Maria is a fascinating process, inevitable from the time Maria first expresses her irritation with Thomas. When Anselm first begs her to flee with him, she is speechless; then she tells him that he is crazy.

But by the time Josef and Thomas expose Anselm, her attitude has changed. In an antirational outburst quite rare in Musil's writings Maria tells her husband:

> Perhaps [Anselm] does falsify. But I have a right to have said to me: This is the way it is! That—and even if it were only a deception—there is something growing that is stronger than me. . . . That music leads me, not that someone tells me: Don't forget, here a piece of dried intestine is being scratched! Not because I'm stupid, Thomas, but because I'm a human being! [35]

Anselm's irrationality is for Maria, then, partly an escape from the pitiless rationality of her husband.

At an earlier stage in their relationship Maria accuses Anselm of being "in danger of becoming a bad man." Anselm rejects the moralistic implication of this statement. "Oh, Maria," he says, "I'm less than a bad man; a scholar who has lost his scholarliness, and a man who again and again when a choice had to be made chose the wrong means." [36] And in order to prove to Maria that although he is a coward (which he admits) he can yet be strong, Anselm presses the end of her burning cigarette into his palm. This incident is a prime example of a basic assumption in *The Visionaries*, and indeed in Musil's works generally, that character is never simple or unalloyed. Simplistic judgments, such as Josef's about Anselm, are continually being broken up into kaleidoscopic bits of behavioral relativism. The Machian concept of "functional relationships" seems to have replaced in Musil's thought the more rigid and idealized absolutes of conventional values.

Thomas' feeling toward Anselm progresses from warm friendship through anger and bitter contempt to a realization of his own impotence. The transition to the final stage of this progression is Anselm's sham suicide at the end of the second act. Thomas here has an illumination about Anselm. He tells Maria, who comes in and asks what happened: "He attempted a false suicide. But true feeling and false probably come to the same thing in the end." Regine adds that "there are people who are true behind lies and insincere before the truth," [37] an echo of Anselm's sophistic but serious apology to Maria for his lying: "But lies are the fleeting feeling of being at home in dream-near lands among strange laws; don't you understand? Nearer to the soul, perhaps more honest. Lies aren't true, but otherwise they're everything!" [38]

In summation, Anselm, present or absent, dominates the entire play. Hurtling into the established order of the two households (Josef's and Thomas') of his childhood friends, he has upset the mental checks and balances that had allowed Josef and Regine, and Thomas and Maria, to live with each other in a *modus vivendi.* The implication of this upset is that a *modus vivendi* is not good enough, however much pain may be caused by its dislocation. Anselm's function, unpleasant though both it and he himself may be, is yet felt by the other characters to be necessary as a kind of psychological cathartic. And in facing up to themselves more clearly, they accept Anselm, ultimately, on his own terms.

The presentation of Stader as a comic figure is masterful. The basis of this presentation is irony; Stader takes himself seriously while the audience is allowed to feel superior to his unconsciously clownlike pretensions to "scientific" stature. The proprietor of the detective bureau of Newton, Galileo, and Stader might best be described as seriocomic in relation to the other figures. His position in the economy of the play is basically a serious one; a detective orders and interprets people's external actions, and is hence a behaviorist par excellence. His vocation, that of a kind of lay scientist, depends exclusively on a rationalistic approach to human action. Like Josef, Stader is out of place in Thomas' household. He too tries to apply to the actions of the principals standards which here have no relevance, or rather which do have relevance but not in his terms. It is Stader, for instance, who formulates Mach's theory of functional relationships: "There is no accident! There are no facts! No indeed! There are only—scientific connections!" [39] The statement is comic, but Thomas has spent his life as a scientist investigating "scientific connections" only to realize that without feeling behind them they are not enough. Ulrich in *The Man without Qualities* reaches the logical conclusion of this realization in his utopian ideal of a "Global Secretariat of Exactitude and Soul."

It is difficult to know, the subtle lightnings of Musil's irony being what they are, how serious the character of Stader was intended to be. Josef's remark to Thomas about him may furnish a clue: "You know," Josef says, "the fellow is not a little exaggerated; his scientific method is of course nonsense, but he's clever." [40]

These, then, are the leading characters in this peculiar play. The question arises as to the ultimate pessimism of Musil's view of life as here presented, for the "creative condition," whatever that may be, seems a small dike to erect against the raging sea of dissolving values and relationships in *The Visionaries*. In an ultimate sense one might say that the play is deeply pessimistic; but "pessimistic" and "optimistic" are judgments based essentially on an evaluation of action and character in moral terms. If "good" succumbs to "evil" in a work one might justly speak of pessimism. But as this discussion of *The Visionaries* has brought out, the only such value judgments in the play are delivered by a minor character, Josef, and are satirized in him. Anselm and Maria are not doing a "bad" thing in coming together, but only facing the truth about themselves. In losing their illusions, however, the major figures do not change or develop, but come to realize what they are; and as has been indicated what happens to them is the almost mechanical consequence of what they are. Thomas is excluded in this process as surely and as indifferently as a chemical precipitate in a test tube. It is his awareness of this fact (and who should be better aware of it than a scientist?) that best explains his bitterness.

This is indeed Darwin's struggle of life observed in the social and erotic spheres, and sophisticated and cosmopolitan ones at that; a struggle in which conventional standards of morality are seen as simple-minded. The tragedy of the play, a kind of tragedy of despair, is that Thomas is left alone. Being the kind of person he is, he has to end alone. But in this terrifying Pascalian loneliness is the feeling that it is at least an honest loneliness. Regine too, in announcing her decision to return to Josef, says that she has come to appreciate the meaning of sacrifice.

VI

Vinzenz and the Girl Friend of Important Men

(1924)

Vinzenz and the Girl Friend of Important Men, a farce in three acts, is a comic pendant to *The Visionaries* and is at the same time, in a few respects at least, a precursor of *The Man without Qualities.*

The "girl friend" of the title is "Alpha" (her real name, not revealed until halfway through the play, is Kathi; the pseudonym, with its overtones of primacy and mathematical symbol, was perhaps meant to have an ironic effect). Around her the play revolves. As the farce opens the gruff, rough, and appropriately named merchant Bärli, distracted by his love for Alpha, tries to get her to elope with him. When Alpha, who is cool-headed as well as sensual, refuses, Bärli threatens to shoot her. He is prevented from doing this for the time being by the sudden appearance of Vinzenz from behind a chair. Vinzenz, an insurance actuary who had been Alpha's lover very long ago, has returned to see her. Alpha's other suitors now enter—her whimsicality has led her to bring them together at 3 A.M. to celebrate her birthday. These are a scholar, a musician, a politician, a reformer, a young man, and Alpha's estranged husband, Dr. Apulejus-Halm. Dr. Apulejus-Halm is one of a string of estranged husbands who figure prominently in *The Visionaries*, *Vinzenz*, *Three Women*, and *The Man without Qualities*. The cast is completed by a female friend of Alpha's.

The action of the play consists largely of a series of long dialogues between Vinzenz and Alpha, and also a series of farcical intrigues. The most elaborate of the latter is that staged by Vinzenz in which Bärli finally purges himself of his mad passion for Alpha by "shooting" both Alpha and himself. This action recalls Anselm's sham suicide in *The Visionaries* and has the same overtone: A convincing imitation of a real action can have the same effect as the real action; in the imitation only the physical consequences of the real action are missing. Most of the intrigues in the play are set in motion by Vinzenz himself. At the end of the play he announces his intention of becoming a servant, and Alpha renounces her suitors with the grandiose statement: "You're *all* supremely unimportant to me. For me you're all spiritually dead. Even Vinzenz." [1] She then reveals her intention of divorcing her husband and also becoming a servant.

The two protagonists in *Vinzenz* are far more important than either the plot or the action; indeed the content of the play consists almost entirely of their relationship to each other. Like Maria in *The Visionaries* and Diotima in *The Man without Qualities*, Alpha is the embodiment of sensual attraction. But she is detached as well as coquettish, and she hides her detachment behind an air of not taking other people seriously. Her attachment to Vinzenz, which she has sentimentalized during the fifteen years of their separation, is the only thing in the play that breaks through her veneer. Vinzenz fascinates her because of his constant activity, his shady past, and his marginal position in society. Alpha is especially dazzled by the prospect of unlimited power promised by Vinzenz' wild scheme to make money through a gambling game. One might say that Alpha is chiefly fascinated by Vinzenz as a Musilian man of possibility.

Like Anselm and Regine in *The Visionaries,* Alpha considers herself an anarchist. (The provisional title of *The Visionaries* was *The Anarchists.*) "You mustn't belittle me on account of the people you've seen here," she tells Vinzenz; "I've tried in different directions, but I've never taken them seriously. You know, I believe I'm really an anarchist: they've never stilled the longing in me finally to find my proper place." [2]

In spite of her quaint conception of anarchy, Alpha is thus seeking a "proper place" in the scheme of things. She and Vinzenz are typical of Musil's people in that they think they can overcome their individual isolation if only they could find some magic position in or out of the social hierarchy, some career or husband or wife—or in *The Man without Qualities* some utopia—that is waiting for them. If they could find this position, they seem to think, they would drop into a slot and somehow complete a natural order of things.

The idea in this context is a curious one, and it is perhaps important that it should in this play be presented comically. For we not only saw much the same feeling in Regine and Thomas and in a different way in Stader in *The Visionaries,* but we are also to see the culmination of it in Ulrich in

The Man without Qualities. This feeling of not being at home in the world is not merely a comic pose on Alpha's part, for when the distracted Bärli, waving in her face a pistol neither of them knows to be loaded only with blanks, asks her: "According to what principles do you regulate your actions?" Alpha, a good Musilian even in the face of death, protests: "You can't put it so simply!! It depends!! It's according!!" [3]

Alpha's attitude toward her husband Halm recalls that of Regine toward Josef in *The Visionaries* and foreshadows that between Agathe and her husband in *The Man without Qualities.* Halm is rather like Josef; describing himself as an "art-writer," he reveals his pedantry.[4] But Halm's feeling for Alpha, like Josef's for Regine, is genuine, and his description of her is almost the very same as Josef's description of Regine; he notes her coolness in love and that she has "something wonderfully boylike" about her.[5]

Vinzenz is one of Musil's most curious characters. He is in one sense a comic transposition of Thomas (in *The Visionaries*) to a lower social and mental plane, and he is comic in the way in which Beaumarchais' Figaro and Mann's Felix Krull are comic: a serious thread is interwoven in the comic fabric of his actions. Life sits more easily on Vinzenz than it does on Thomas; Vinzenz is not committed to his work as an insurance actuary as Thomas is committed to his scientific work. Vinzenz can take it or leave it, and in the end decides to leave it. He says at the end of the play:

If one does not find one's own life, one has to go after a strange one. And there the best thing is not to do it out of enthusiasm, but for money. There are only two possibilities for an ambitious man: to create a great work or to become a servant. For the first I'm too honorable; for the second I'm just adequate enough.[6]

"If one does not find one's own life . . .": like all Musil's major figures, Vinzenz is estranged from life. He makes a point of mocking everything that other people take seriously, notably the bourgeois values of Bärli and those of Halm. His fantastic gambling scheme, his arranging Bärli's cathartic "murder" and "suicide" are symptomatic of the Musilian man of possibility, the man who plays with reality because besides things as they are he can imagine another set of things which are not but could just as well be. Alpha accuses Vinzenz: "It's clear that you're the incarnation of a fantastic liar!" to which Vinzenz replies: "Agreed! But what is lying? Maintaining about something desirable that it is the case, instead of it should be the case?" In the same vein he continues: "A fantastic liar is that liar whose lies agree with the facts! For facts are fantastic!" [7]

Behind this sophistic detachment of Vinzenz lurks a refusal to commit himself or accept the world; he refuses Alpha's sincerely offered love, and by swindling and deceiving people flaunts his "outsideness" of reality. Chapter 4 of *The Man without Qualities* contains an explicit and systematic discussion of what it means to be a "man of possibility"; this will be brought up again in a discussion of the novel. But more exactly than any character in Musil's earlier works, except Anselm and possibly Thomas in *The Visionaries*, Vinzenz prefigures Musil's ultimate man of possibility, Ulrich.

A great deal is made of the affinities and tensions between Vinzenz and Alpha, which clearly foreshadow those between Agathe and Ulrich. Alpha tells her friend that "he is a person whom nothing can bind. Like me." [8] At a later point Vinzenz tells Alpha: "Give me your hand [*he reaches out his hand to her*]. It's really tried me, this reunion with my soul." [9] And in the last line of the play Vinzenz refuses Alpha's suggestion that as servants they work in the same house: "No, I was about to ask you to go into some other house; we are perhaps too much alike." [10]

Perhaps this polarity between the two like-minded title figures is the most important aspect of *Vinzenz and the Girl Friend of Important Men.* This type of relationship, previously seen in Thomas and Regine in *The Visionaries*, was to become one of the central frames of reference of *The Man without Qualities.* In the novel the couple is no longer a brother and sister-in-law, or a married woman and her former lover, but a natural brother and sister whose physical and metaphysical incest is the final step in Musil's representation of the spiritual union between the man and woman of possibility.

VII

Three Women (1924)

THE strongest impression gained from these three stories, first published in 1924, is that of experimentation. Musil here seems to be trying different literary forms as vehicles for the expression of his view of life. The forms of these virtuoso pieces are traditional, but of widely differing types; their importance in the frame of Musil's work as a whole is as the final stage of crystallization of his thought and themes before *The Man without Qualities*. An important piece of circumstantial evidence supporting this view of *Three Women* as primarily exercises in form is the swarm of similar stories by other authors that each calls to mind. Where Musil's other works seem to defy easy comparison with anyone else's, these stories almost demand it. In this sense they are traditional. Whether there is any definite connection between these stories and the works of others cannot be determined on the basis of the scanty evidence presently available, but comparisons often suggest themselves.

The assumption underlying these stories may be stated as follows: Place a man and a woman who are attracted to each other in a limited situation against a sharply defined background (the backgrounds of the stories are quite different from each other) and, given their characters, try to make them act and react consistently. There are in all three pieces at least overtones of violence, of some threat to life; death intrudes as a result of the appearance in a character of the will to die. It is principally this death-wish that kills Homo in "Grigia" and Tonka in "Tonka," and nearly kills Herr von Ketten in "The Portuguese Lady." How this death-wish arises and develops is the psychological nucleus around which each of the stories is built.

Other factors common to the three stories have been mentioned in Chapter II. These include the location of all three works in border regions, the differing nationalities of the members of the individual couples in all three, and also the striking fact that the three women in their respective stories all act as passive agents who bring the male figures to a new realization of themselves. That Musil's otherwise saturating irony is largely absent from *Three Women* further supports the argument that these stories are exercises rather than attempts at ultimate statement.

"*Grigia*"

Like Musil's earlier story "The Completion of Love," "Grigia" is set in motion by separation, in this case the separation of the geologist Homo from a life of habit and responsibility represented by a wife and sick son. Homo is called to northern Italy by an acquaintance, whimsically named Mozart Amadeo Hoffingott, to help open up an old mine. The region is a peculiar and primitive one, peopled long ago by Germans; the natives speak a degenerated German dialect. Driven by an obscure death-wish Homo takes up with a cowgirl whom he nicknames "Grigia" after one of her cows. (Musil's consistent use of female pseudonyms often seems to be more a whimsical gesture than a serious questioning of identity.) Eventually they are sealed in an abandoned mine adit by Grigia's jealous husband. Grigia escapes, but Homo starves to death.

The peculiar resemblances to Hemingway in this story are best explained biographically, since *Three Women* appeared a year before Hemingway's first great success, *The Sun Also Rises*. Musil too, as a captain in the Austrian army during the First World War, saw action in the Italian campaign. His war diaries contain several incidents which are used almost verbatim in "Grigia" (the description of dynamiting, the sudden sight in the dark of a white peak illuminated by the moon and a searchlight, the death of a fly). In their precise and dispassionate description, these are to be compared to the tone and atmosphere of *A Farewell to Arms* (1929).

The first paragraph of "Grigia" sets up the whole story. It is significant that Musil begins by stating a general principle of which the story itself is an illustration. "There is a time in life," the story begins, "when life slows down surprisingly, as if it hesitated to go on or wanted to change its direction. It may be that during this time a misfortune may more easily overtake one." [1] Homo's mood at the beginning of the story is one of dissociation and isolation. He rejects a rest cure for his malaise because "it seemed to him that [he] would thus be separated too long from himself, from his books, his plans, and his life." [2] Homo had never before been separated from his wife, although their son had come between them "like a stone into which water has trickled and is driving farther and farther apart." [3]

Like other of Musil's characters, notably Ulrich in *The*

Man without Qualities, Homo is overtaken "in the middle of the path of our life" by a malaise that changes the direction of his life. Freed from social restraints at this dangerous time by his transplantation to the primitive world of the story, Homo's personality gradually dissolves and precipitates his death. Significantly, this process of dissolution is well under way *before* Homo meets Grigia, who is thus shown to be an accidental factor in the situation. It is remarkable in all Musil's writings how rarely one figure is directly affected by another; the changes resulting from contacts between characters are always shown to have originated in the psyche of the person affected. The second person acts like a photographic developer, which can only bring out a latent image already present in the negative.

It would be tedious to trace the numerous signs that show Homo freeing himself in this new environment from the protective restraints of his former life. His freedom from restraint and his preoccupation with death increase at a corresponding rate. From the day on which the nonreligious Homo feels a mystical certainty of reunion after death, apparently with his wife, he feels his love for her to be pure, and from this day on he is freed from "the connection to wanting to be alive, from horror in the face of death." [4] This sinister note in the story, handled with remarkable virtuosity, becomes insistent.

The whole atmosphere of "Grigia" is superbly summed up in an image Musil uses to describe the landscape of the region in May: "Because the trees did not discard their foliage, the faded and the new were interwoven as in cemetery wreaths." [5] It should be noted in passing that Musil's evocation of both milieu in general and landscape in particular is very powerful; the overtones of Stifter in this connection, and those of Novalis in the mystic evocation of ores and minerals are not, perhaps, accidental. The story of Homo's decline and fall is not merely set against this background; as in so many of Stifter's stories the action grows organically out of the background.

The milieu of "Grigia" includes an impression of the decadence of the cosmopolitan European society the imported miners have left behind. This is sharply portrayed in the frustrated boredom of their evenings in this remote world close to nature, evenings spent in dancing to erotic popular music and in quarreling with Hemingwayesque futility. (Musil's characters have far more psychological depth than Hemingway's, and in addition their futility is a transitional stage between a *modus vivendi* and a catastrophe, while Hemingway's characters seem to live in a permanent kind of *status quo;* so the parallel must be hedged about. Still, the similarity of impression remains.) Musil's transplantation of one kind of social mores into a context in which it does not belong has in it something of fatality as well as futility. Even the death of a poisoned fly contributes to the growing feeling of incipient disaster. Homo observes the fly intently: "But when death came, the dying fly folded its six little legs quite sharply together and held them that way in the air; then it died in its pale spot of light on the oilcloth as if in a cemetery of silence that was not to be measured in centimeters, and was not for ears, but still was there." [6] Homo snaps the dead fly into the face of a retired Major sitting opposite. The next paragraph begins: "At that time he had long since made the acquaintance of Grigia," [7] and the story begins its well-prepared fall to catastrophe.

Grigia is as wild and primitive as her fellow creatures in their isolated primitive home. She looked, we are told, "as naturally lovely as a slender poisonous mushroom," [8] and the omniscient author tells us later in describing Homo's impression of Grigia:

There remained always contained in this impression something of a horror of nature, and one should not deceive oneself: Nature is by no means "natural"; in everything in which man has not imposed his restraint on it, it is earthy, edged, poisonous and inhuman. It was apparently just this that bound [Homo] to the peasant girl, and for the rest a never-weary astonishment because she so much resembled a lady. One would also be surprised if one saw an elegant matron sitting in a wood with a teacup.[9]

After Homo conquers Grigia sexually the catastrophe follows with extreme rapidity. (Grigia is not introduced until the story is three-fifths over, and the actual catastrophe occurs in the last few pages; this further emphasizes Grigia's subordinate role in the process of Homo's disintegration.) Homo's death-wish now comes to the surface; he "felt somehow that he would soon die, only he did not know how, or when. His old life had become powerless; it became like a butterfly which toward autumn grows weaker and weaker." [10] Grigia suddenly calls their affair off, but Homo disregards her warnings and forces her to go with him to an old mine. Here her husband rolls a boulder in front of the entrance, and Homo feels that his fate is consummated in a grotesque love-death. For a long time the two lie together in the darkness, growing weaker. Then Homo wakes up to find Grigia gone and sees the light distantly glimmering through a side crevice through which she must have escaped. It is significant that he had not looked for an exit earlier; perhaps his death-wish had become too strong. Homo thinks he can also escape through this opening, "but he was at this moment perhaps already too weak to turn back to life, did not want to, or had become faint" [11]

—the author scrupulously avoids putting an interpretation upon this final lack of action. At this same hour Hoffingott calls off the unsuccessful geological project.

This study of dissolution and rush toward death shows Musil's skill in handling dramatic narrative, a skill in which the reader of *The Man without Qualities* might think him deficient. That Musil used in his most ambitious work another technique out of choice and not because he was incapable of writing dramatically in a more conventional form is an indication of the extent of his talent. This dramatic skill is used in "Grigia" to make a point that Yeats has stated most succinctly in "Oedipus at Colonus," that "delight becomes death-longing, if all longing else be vain."

"*The Portuguese Lady*"

Musil's diaries of the period about 1916–1918 contain a reference to Shelley's *Cenci*,[12] and the romantic world of this play is the setting of the second of these stories, which also calls to mind Tieck, Hawthorne, and Poe. "The Portuguese Lady" might be called a "tale" in the sense in which these writers understood the term.

The first paragraph of the story establishes the position of the feudal family of Von Ketten, or Delle Catene, between north and south (the name "Chains" can hardly be accidental). They live austere lives, directed by will and ambition, in complete isolation in their remote mountain fastness. They share a family fate: hair early streaked with white and death before sixty. It has been the custom of this family to seek wives from distant lands in order to avoid pacts and feuds with their neighbors; in this and other ways the element of isolation in this story is very heavily emphasized. The basic characterization in this story is of the family; the particular Herr von Ketten here presented is seen as a typical representative of his line. In the early pages the characteristics of this lord are constantly referred to those of all the Von Kettens, as for instance in the statement that when they went off to seek their brides they all became, for the one year of their absence, dazzling cavaliers. The family has been involved in a long-drawn-out feud with the bishops of Trento, and the wars engendered by this feud are an important mechanism in the story.

The Portuguese lady comes into this forbidding world as the bride of the present Herr von Ketten. Her first sight of her new home calls forth the most powerful description in all Musil's works:

Wild stieg das Schloss auf. Da und dort sassen an der Felsbrust verkümmerte Bäumchen wie einzelne Haare. Die Waldberge stürzten so auf und nieder, dass man diese Hässlichkeit einem, der nur die Meereswellen kannte, gar nicht hätte zu beschreiben vermögen. Voll kaltgewordener Würze war die Luft, und alles war so, als ritte man in einen grossen zerborstenen Topf hinein, der eine fremde grüne Farbe enthielt. . . . Unergründete Schluchten boten den Drachen Aufenthalt. Wochenweit und -tief war der Wald, durch den nur die Wildfährten führten . . . ; nie führte eines Christen Weg hinauf, und wann es aus Fürwitz geschehen war, hatte es Widerfahrnisse zur Folge, von denen die Mägde in den Winterstuben mit leiser Stimme berichteten, während die Knechte geschmeichelt schwiegen und die Schulter hochzogen, weil das Männerleben gefährlich ist und solche Abenteuer einem darin zustossen können.

("Wild rose up the castle. Here and there stunted little trees sat on the breast of rock like single hairs. The wooded mountains rushed up and down in such a way that one would not have been able to describe this ugliness to a person who knew only the waves of the sea. Full of chilled spices was the air, and everything was as if one were to ride into a large burst pot containing a strange green color. . . . Unsounded abysses offered dragons abode. Weeks broad and deep was the forest, through which only the tracks of wild animals led . . . ; never did the path of a Christian lead there, but if, out of inquisitiveness, it had happened, it had had as a consequence occurrences of which the maidservants in winter rooms reported in low voice, while the menservants, flattered, were silent and shrugged their shoulders because a man's life is dangerous, and such adventures could befall one in it.") [13]

But what strikes its new mistress most about her home is that there are so many stone walls. The lord spends two days with his bride, to whom he is devoted, and then rides away to carry on the fight against the bishops. Eleven years later, one year before the time of the story, he is still fighting. His patient, devoted and long-suffering wife reflects in her own way his stubborn endurance. In his brief moments at home the lord has sired two sons and collected the rudiments of culture for his wife's pleasure. Von Ketten and his wife have no spontaneous communication with each other, and yet subtly feel themselves one.

The feud is finally settled and Von Ketten finds the purpose gone from his life. On his way home he is bitten on the hand by a fly and contracts a mysterious wasting fever. He resigns himself to dying, but changes his mind on the day he realizes that unless he summons all his will power he will die; and "that was the day in the evening of which the fever sank." [14] But for weeks he is completely helpless. A soothsayer tells him: "You will only be cured when you accomplish something." [15] The course of this illness implies a psychic and perhaps symbolic origin of the physical disease.

A countryman of the wife comes to visit, and she is revivified by this contact with her native culture. The countryman apparently falls in love with her, which arouses the jealousy of the helpless lord.

A mysterious cat that acts like a human being makes its appearance at the castle. It grows weak, and its illness is described with the same clinical precision as was that of Herr von Ketten. The cat has a halo, and in case anyone should miss the point we are told:

> One would not have felt this wasting away so strangely in a human being, but in the animal it was as if it were becoming a human being. They looked at it almost with reverence; none of these three people [Von Ketten, his wife, and her countryman], in his particular situation, was spared the thought that it was his own fate which had been transferred to this small cat, already half released from earthly cares.[16]

The cat is finally killed to put it out of its misery.

Von Ketten suddenly remembers a childhood ambition to climb the incredibly steep cliff on which his castle sits. The resolve is suicidal, and somehow connected with the dead cat: "Not he, but the little cat from the Beyond would come this way, it seemed to him." [17] One night he awakens to find himself a third of the way up the cliff. The ensuing struggle with death restores his strength (thus fulfilling the soothsayer's prophecy), and he succeeds.

As a result of this struggle Von Ketten achieves an obscure spiritual reunion with his wife. The final paragraph reads: " 'If God could become a man, he can also become a cat,' said the Portuguese Lady, and he would have had to hold his hand over her mouth on account of the blasphemy; but they both knew that no syllable of it forced itself out of these walls."[18] The wife's countryman had previously departed quite suddenly, forestalling Von Ketten's plan to kill him.

As in "Grigia" the main focus of attention in this story is the chief male figure; the Portuguese lady is static. Her situation is the opposite of Grigia's; the latter was part of her environment and received a stranger, while the Portuguese lady is the stranger who is received into the man's environment, the environment in both cases being a small pocket of life completely cut off from the reality of the stranger's former life.

"The Portuguese Lady" is unique among Musil's works in that its central concern is not the consideration of problems of character or of ideas, but the establishment of mood; family and setting are more important than the individual characters, who are seen from a strictly external point of view. The Herr von Ketten of this story is not the self-haunted hero that we find in Musil's major works, *The Confusions of Young Törless, The Visionaries*, and *The Man without Qualities*, or in most of his minor ones including both "Grigia" and "Tonka." "The Portuguese Lady" must consequently be read as a beautiful experiment in a specific genre, that of the Romantic tale, rather than as an analysis of the workings of the mind.

"*Tonka*"

This is the longest of the stories in *Three Women* and the one that has the most connections—though they are not many—with Musil's earlier and later works. As in "Grigia" a critical moment in the life of the chief male figure is the seed crystal around which the story forms. The unnamed middle-class hero of the story falls in love with a poor and inarticulate girl, Tonka, during "his military year. . . . One is never so denuded of oneself and one's own works as at this time of life. . . . One is less protected at this time than otherwise." [19] The man narrates the story in the third person. That he is no longer sure of the events shows that he is recalling the distant past, and the atmosphere of the story is one of distant detachment.

The plot itself is hackneyed: boy with socially conscious mother loves poor girl, takes her for his mistress; she dies bearing a child he denies is his, and he is matured by the shattering experience. If one thinks back to Musil's earlier story "The Completion of Love," one can see how much of a literary exercise "Tonka" is. And more than the plot of this story is commonplace: the simple Czech girls—the setting is a Czech city—loved by German boys of higher station abound in the literature of the time, apparently a reflection of the milieu. Class distinction is, for the only time in Musil's works, an important source of conflict, and it is used in a conventionally literary way. The hero's mother tries to buy off the girl and goes to great lengths to break up an affair which she thinks improper for her son from a social standpoint. In addition to this the shabby clothes, shabby rooms, shabby people, and shabby urban scenery all contribute to a conventionally literary impression of faded *fin-de-siècle* decadence without parallel in Musil's works except for the decadent boredom of the motley crew of geologists in the primitive setting of "Grigia." In contrast to the exotic settings of its companion stories the urban environment of "Tonka" is depressing in its actuality; above the story hover the spirits of Zola and Schnitzler.

What is not trite in "Tonka" is the style. Clear and precise, it is the style which lifts this story above the tired elements of which it is composed. The few impressionistic images reinforce the detached clarity of this style. An excellent example of this occurs near the end of the story: "He noticed how good he still had it, who could express himself, and Tonka couldn't. And in this moment he recognized her quite clearly. She was a snowflake that falls alone in the middle of a summer day. But in the next moment this was no explanation at all, and perhaps too she was simply a good girl." [20] For clear transparency of style "Tonka" stands out among all Musil's works.

"Tonka" is also to some extent an experiment in point of view. This problem in the story may be put as follows: how to describe a simple and inarticulate girl long since dead through the eyes of the man who had brought her to death. The answer is the process of retrospection on the part of the man himself; narrative in the third person creates a feeling of partial impersonality, and the softened edges of reminiscence blur the sordidness of the action.

Although Tonka is the center of attention in the story, her role in the development of the man who is recording it is a passive one. Her real name was Antonie; "Tonka" was an abbreviation of her Czech nickname. Tonka was a natural and unimpressive girl; her face had, "without being beautiful, something clear and distinct. Nothing in it had that small artfully feminine quality that works only through arrangement: mouth, nose, eyes, each feature stood clearly for itself, and could bear to be observed for itself, without charming through anything but its frankness and the freshness which was poured over the whole." [21] This is not description at all, but rather a sympathetic impression—an indication of Musil's skill in handling point of view. Tonka "was not stupid, but something seemed to prevent her from being clever." [22] The man, trying to break through her inarticulateness, laughs in saying: "That's something that's never happened to me: not to be able to say something!" [23] The major conflict in the story is between his education and articulateness, on the one hand, and Tonka's ignorance and inarticulateness, on the other. A subordinate conflict is the social struggle indicated above in which the man opposes his mother.

Tonka defies her lover's attempts to educate and improve her: "She remained like nature, pure and uncut. It was not at all so simple to love the simple girl." [24]

Tonka conceives a child during the lover's absence, and somehow contracts a venereal disease; she refuses to say anything about it, although remaining as attached to her lover as ever. A vaguely allegorical tinge is noticeable here, although it is somewhat less obvious than the mysterious cat in "The Portuguese Lady"; Tonka's face assumes the expression of the world of the Virgin Mary and Pontius Pilate.[25] Her illness progressively worsens in the absolute poverty in which they are forced to live while the man completes his studies. He had never had either the time or the inclination for friendships, and while sticking by Tonka he feels more and more his isolation from the world. To all his attempts to discover the father of the child Tonka replies: "Send me away if you don't want to believe me." [26]

The man's isolation becomes poignant: "When one does not look at the world with the eyes of the world, but has it already in his glance, it falls into meaningless details that live separated from each other as sadly as stars in the night." [27] The man is also moved to a Stendhalian reflection that has occurred in similar form in Musil's earlier works, notably *The Confusions of Young Törless* and *The Visionaries:* "It is not the loved one that is the origin of the feelings which are apparently aroused through her, but these are placed behind her like a light. . . . He could not bring himself to place the light behind Tonka." [28] Although he has long since come to believe in the dying Tonka, he cannot bring himself to tell her so. He writes her long letters when she is in the hospital, but never sends them. When she dies, he goes on to a promising career with the consciousness that something is finished. At the end we are told:

> And much occurred to him since then that made him somewhat better than others because a small warm shadow lay on his brilliant life. That was no longer of any help to Tonka. But it helped him. Even if human life flows by too quickly for a person to be able to hear each one of its voices and find the response to it.[29]

This rather odd conclusion, that the narrator uses his experience as a step to the Parnassus of self-realization, is justified in terms of the story only because the narrator is never really emotionally attached to Tonka. His conduct toward her is motivated chiefly by a sense of duty—the same sense of duty that his mother feels toward his sick father. And how could it be otherwise? The man and Tonka live on different levels and never understand one another; thus he can be presented as not being destroyed by the experience that destroys her. There is in this insistence on individuals being separated from each other by living on different planes a strong echo of *The Confusions of Young Törless.*

The narrator of this story is a familiar Musilian figure. He is a scientist at the beginning of his career who, throughout his poverty and involvement with Tonka, works on an invention that is later to make him famous; even when he is a struggling student people come to see him about his work. In many ways he suggests Thomas in *The Visionaries* at an early stage of development. As Thomas had in his youth believed in a new life to be brought about by scientific advances, so does this man believe that "after this time, which destroys as much as it builds, a time will come which has the new assumptions we are creating with such asceticism, and only then will one know what one should have felt." [30] This same kind of march toward some future utopia was to preoccupy the hero of *The Man without Qualities.*

Three Women might better have been called *Three Men.* For even in "Tonka" the woman is only an accessory in the acquisition by a man of a more complete self-realization. To be sure all three women deflect and influence this realization in varying degrees, but they are very much passive agents in the active development—or, in "Grigia," disintegration—of the men with whose lives they come in contact. But in these stories both men and women are subordinate to mood and setting. Musil's ability to evoke these qualities with power is one of his most brilliant accomplishments. In addition, for sheer beauty of language "The Portuguese Lady" is matched only by certain passages in the unfinished third part of *The Man without Qualities.*

In comparison with his first novel and earlier stories, Musil in *Three Women* sharpened the precision of his language and laid more emphasis on form. Here the psychologist and moralist has stepped back in favor of the storyteller.

To compare *Three Women* to *The Man without Qualities* is to compare a pilot fish swimming unconcernedly in front of a shark with the shark. It would be regrettable if Musil's great second novel completely overshadowed the haunting beauty of the small book which immediately preceded it.

VIII

The Man without Qualities

(1930-1952)

SINCE the Renaissance men have made various attempts to systematize human knowledge and, by integrating this knowledge with the private lives of individuals, to achieve a reconciliation of the inner and outer life of man which will replace the dominant religious faith of earlier times. One of the most interesting of these attempts, generally stronger on the integration than on the systematization of knowledge, is to be found in the encyclopedic novels of the late nineteenth and early twentieth centuries. In these novels essays, commentaries, and theories on a vast scale are imbedded in the fabric of an ambitious fictional reconstruction of the world. By including a great variety of man's knowledge and experience the writers of these novels show a more serious purpose than simply to entertain. They are searching for a pattern that will explain, or at least enable man to order, the whole of life; a pattern that will reconcile man and the world around him. Since the modern Western world has no single scale of accepted values, the authors of *War and Peace*, *Remembrance of Things Past*, *Ulysses*, *The Magic Mountain*, and *The Man without Qualities* had to work with scales of value of their own choosing. Tolstoy chose the scale of historical process; Proust that of art; Joyce and Musil that of myth; and Mann a scale of eclectic values built around a framework of humanism.

The authors of these encyclopedic novels, then, were searching with great urgency through art, each in his own way, for a comprehensive unity in the life of man. "In the life of man" is a most important qualifying phrase, for one of the few empirically deducible principles of the novel as a genre is that it is set in the real world, or a convincing analogue of it. The novelist is committed to presenting a picture of what could be daily life, and the very fact that the authors of the works referred to above chose to write novels rather than essays or philosophical treatises is most important. It committed them to a presentation of man in the social context in which, from day to day, he lives.

Thus these writers, in these particular works at least, may be called humanists in that man is at the center of their view of the world. Whatever they were searching for through their novels was designed to make man whole, complete, and happy in this life, not another. And this search was a serious one. That these writers exploded the boundaries of the novel as conventionally conceived in the eighteenth and nineteenth centuries by including in their works much that lies entirely outside the realm of art demonstrates, I think, the urgency of their quest. A purely fictional vehicle alone was insufficient for their purposes.

It has often been maintained that a work of art does something more than mirror reality, that it creates a reality of its own, which then has an existence of its own. This idea is of great importance for the novelist—especially for the novelist, since among all artists, with the possible exception of the dramatist, he is the one most dependent on the specific social conditions of a specific society. The lyric poet, the painter, and the musician have much more freedom in interpreting the world than the novelist does. But if the novelist creates a picture of the real world which is in itself a second reality, this puts a powerful weapon into his hands, especially if he is a novelist whose central concern is to point the way toward a whole, complete, and happy life. He can use this second reality as contrast: he can point to his "raw material," the world as it is and man as he is, and rework both in the direction of an ideal reality, the world as it should be and man as he should be. Stendhal's image for the novel was of a mirror carried along a highway, at one moment reflecting puddles in the road, at another the azure sky. But I think that with any novel which is the work of a superior and intense imagination a closer look at this jouncing mirror will reveal a painting with a mirror surface, even if the painting is sometimes not easy to see through the reflection.

If a novelist whose central concern is to point the way toward an ideal life uses both the real world and the "painting" which reflects the real world but is at the same time independent of it, is there not a danger of his becoming didactic? It seems to me that every work of art is in some sense didactic; the danger is that, in the present case, the novelist might start from the wrong end and say: This is the whole, complete, and happy life; and here is the way to get there. The authors of *War and Peace*, *Remembrance of Things Past*, *Ulysses*, *The Magic Mountain*, and *The Man without Qualities* start from the other end, with the awareness and belief that there must be an ideal life. Their central practical concern is how to get there; the goal itself—which always seems to be indistinct—concerns them less than the means of reaching it, of making the changes necessary in daily life and habits of thinking in order to prepare the ground for an eventual utopia.

Of all these encyclopedic novels, which stand as a group sharply apart from the novels that preceded or have followed them, the tardiest to achieve recognition has been Robert Musil's *The Man without Qualities*. The burden of this chapter will be an attempt to indicate the basic values upon which this enormous work is built, leading up to a discussion of some of the novel's characters as embodiments of these values.

I

The Man without Qualities opens with a weather report for the continent of Europe of a day in the month of August, 1913. This is the setting, and this the time, of a novel that might be called without exaggeration the spiritual biography of an age and of an empire, and the spiritual autobiography and utopian vision of a man. The age is our own; the empire is Austria-Hungary, and the man is Robert Musil. It is around these poles that this huge work is oriented.

In the early part of the twentieth century it was clear that the discoveries of science were outdistancing man's adjustment to living in a scientific world. It was a period in which man's moral core, his belief in the integrity of his qualities as an individual, seemed crushed by the ubiquitous impersonality of an efficient, mechanical technology (an aspect of the period eloquently summed up in the movies of Charlie Chaplin)—a period which kept the forms of earlier times in its architecture, its political institutions and social organization, but which seemed to have lost their content. One result of these displacements was the cutting of links between one individual and another, as well as of those between the individual and the world around him. Musil writes:

In earlier times one could be an individual with a better conscience than one can today. People used to be like the stalks of corn in the field. They were probably more violently flung to and fro by God, hail, fire, pestilence and war than they are today, but it was collectively, in terms of towns, of countrysides, the field as a whole; and whatever was left to the individual stalk in the way of personal movement was something that could be answered for and was clearly defined. Today, on the other hand, responsibility's point of gravity lies not in the individual but in the relations between things. Has one not noticed that experiences have made themselves independent of man? . . . Who today can still say that his anger is really his own anger, with so many people butting in and knowing so much more about it than he does? There has arisen a world of qualities without a man to them, of experiences without anyone to experience them, and it almost looks as though under ideal conditions man would no longer experience anything at all privately and the comforting weight of personal responsibility would dissolve into a system of formulae for potential meanings. It is probable that the dissolution of the anthropocentric attitude (an attitude that, after so long seeing man as the centre of the universe, has been dissolving for some centuries now) has finally begun to affect the personality itself; for the belief that the most important thing about experience is the experiencing of it, and about deeds the doing of them, is beginning to strike most people as naive.[1]

For Musil this disjointed age finds its ideal reflection in that patchwork quilt of an empire, Austria-Hungary; "Kakania, that misunderstood State that has since vanished," [2] in which "one was negatively free, constantly aware of the inadequate grounds for one's own existence and lapped by the great fantasy of all that had not happened, or at least had not yet irrevocably happened, as by the foam of the oceans from which mankind arose." [3] Musil's portrait of this land is bathed in a gentle and affectionate irony. Even while limning its incredibility he betrays both a love and a regret for it which are conspicuously absent from other important aspects of the novel, a love and regret, tinged by the melancholy of exile, for a land that no longer exists.

By calling *The Man without Qualities* a "spiritual autobiography" I hope to avoid the booby trap that one springs by falling back on the literally autobiographical details of a work of art. There are many such details, even themes and characters, in this novel; but surely the use to which they are put is more important than the question of their origin. And in this work the autobiographical elements are part of a larger and more important pattern. For Musil has taken his own attitudes, situation, and experience as representative for the man of intellect in the world that Bernard Shaw called Heartbreak House. By presenting what was typical and general in himself (as well as by freely inventing many qualities that were alien to him) he created the portrait of a man whose admirable qualities were paralyzed by the age in which he lived, a man who takes a "year's leave" from life to take stock of his own life.

Finding it impossible to accomplish anything in this age, Ulrich, the chief character of the novel, lowers the sights of his ambition:

His view was that in this century we and all humanity are on an expedition, that pride requires that all useless questionings should be met with a "not yet," and that life should be conducted on interim principles, though in the consciousness of a destination that will be reached by those who come after us.

The sentence that follows sharpens the utopian direction of this thought, and is also remarkable for its echo of Nietzsche:

The truth is that science has developed a conception of hard, sober intellectual strength that makes mankind's old metaphysical and moral notions simply unendurable, although all it can put in their place is the hope that a day, still distant, will come when a race of intellectual conquerors will descend into the valleys of spiritual fruitfulness.[4]

Behind this statement and behind Ulrich's eventual withdrawal from the world lies a deeper fear, a fear which is no less terrible for having become commonplace today. Malcolm Cowley, writing in *The Literary Situation* about the "new" American writers of the 1950's, has expressed it typically:

I think the real background of their work is a sort of horror at what is happening in the world—not a specialized horror at any one development like atomic weapons, totalitarian governments, the cold war, or the restrictions on personal liberty in all countries, but rather a generalized dismay at the results of five centuries of progress and widening enlightenment. Men have outrun themselves; their technical knowledge has increased so much more rapidly than their moral judgment and self-control and simple kindness—if these have increased at all—that the knowledge might destroy them as a species. . . . Combined with the fear of catastrophe is the feeling that individuals are unable to prevent it.[5]

Musil has succeeded in expressing this feeling through art in such a way that, although he could not have anticipated atomic weapons and ballistic missiles, these later developments only extend his thought, like new variations added to a theme in music. At the bottom of his thought lies a passionate moral concern about the dissolution of all meaningful human bonds and values.

The lack of unity in the modern world is the theme of *The Man without Qualities.* "There is no longer a whole man confronting a whole world," Ulrich tells his friend Walter, "but a human something floating about in a universal culture-medium." [6] This statement is typical of those to be found on almost every page of the novel. This lack of unity, which amounts to what might be called a "Humpty-Dumpty complex" (with Ulrich cast in the role of the King's men), is far from static; this atomized world is rushing with brimming energy, like a stellar constellation, toward some terrible unknown goal. That this energy is leading toward war forms one of the many ironies of the novel, for this fact, which the reader can hardly forget or overlook, is unknown to the people in the book. Musil points out, in typically relativistic fashion:

> The train of events is a train unrolling its rails ahead of itself. The river of time is a river sweeping its banks along with it. The traveller moves about on a solid floor between solid walls; but the floor and the walls are being moved along too, imperceptibly, and yet in very lively fashion, by the movements that his fellow-travellers make. . . . The days rocked from side to side, running into weeks. The weeks did not stand still, but wreathed together into chains.[7]

Lack of unity as a theme permeates *The Man without Qualities.* It is evident on many levels, in the method and style as well as in the themes and characters. The image of the kaleidoscope explains this novel as none other can; *The*

Man without Qualities is a picture of a kaleidoscopic world ("men are types, their thoughts, feelings are types," Musil wrote in an early study for the novel, "only the kaleidoscope changes" [8]). The atomized language, the dissolving acid of irony, the fragmentation and isolation of character, and the deliberate breaking-down of the narrative technique—which, like the flight of Zeno's arrow, is split up into "units"—are just as much manifestations of the lack of unity in our time as are the frequent discussions of it in the work. Even Arnheim, the great industrialist and popular philosopher modeled on Walther Rathenau, who thinks he represents a new synthesis—and he does, but a false one—can be overwhelmed by "the feeling that he had forgotten some path he had originally been following, and that the whole of the ideology of the great man (with which he had been filled) was only the emergency substitute for something he had lost." [9] But the compartmentalized world remains an obstacle for Ulrich, the man of intellect who is sincerely seeking to unify through thought the elements of life; and more even than an obstacle it is the thorn in his flesh which drives him on in his search for a new morality:

> Values have been shifted round. Certain questions have been taken out of man's heart. What has been set up for the breeding of high-flying thoughts is a kind of poultry-farm known as philosophy, theology or literature, where in their own way they multiply and increase beyond counting; and that is quite convenient, for faced with such expansion nobody any longer needs to reproach himself with not being able to look after them personally.[10]

Lack of unity, then, is the theme of the great fugue of *The Man without Qualities*, and its clear notes can be heard in any discussion of the book. But there is another side to this theme which from Musil's point of view is far more important than the problem of a lack of unity in modern life. This other side, which the whole movement of the novel exemplifies, is an attempt to overcome the fragmentation, in much the same way that Ernst Mach (on whom, it will be remembered, Musil wrote his doctoral dissertation) and J. Robert Oppenheimer envision an eventual unity of all the sciences and beyond that of all thought. It is precisely in this sense that Ulrich's idea of conducting life on "interim principles" in expectation of an eventual ideal unity is to be understood. This movement, this search, unifies Musil's large and apparently formless novel. The world of society and the world of myth are subjected to the great emotional pressure of Ulrich's seeking, and from this the tension of *The Man without Qualities* arises.

This attempt to overcome the fragmentation of life through a search for a new morality leads to an extraordinary paradox. For the whole course of Ulrich's seeking consists of a series of retreats, not advances. He gives up the search for unity through personal accomplishment by successively giving up three professional careers; he gives up the search through social action by giving up the "Collateral Campaign" which is set in motion to plan the celebration of the Emperor's jubilee in 1918. He withdraws to a family relationship, leaving the world to its own devices, and eventually achieves a unity of a most fragile and limited kind on a mystic island in a mythical relationship with his sister, which soon fails. In the obscure late notes and fragments of the unfinished novel he is apparently meant to return to Vienna and war.

Did Musil mean that, in spite of his talk about conducting life on interim principles and contributing toward an eventual unity that someone else will see, it is only by renouncing the world that the man of intellect will be able to retain a sense of his own individual integrity—and that this is more important? Or did he mean Ulrich to be a prophet, going through an almost religious process of turning away from the world in gradual stages and turning toward the self, from which the prophet speaks to mankind? And yet Ulrich is no prophet in this sense; he has no self in this sense and acquires none; he is a child of his time, a "man without qualities," whose life is rather a commentary on an age than a prophetic vision of a new order. How different this is, for instance, from the burning commitment to life of Ivan in *The Brothers Karamazov*, who exclaims:

> I must have justice, or I will destroy myself. And not justice in some remote infinite time and space, but here on earth, and that I could see myself. I have believed in it. I want to see it, and if I am dead by then, let me rise again, for if it all happens without me it will be too unfair. Surely I haven't suffered simply that I, my crimes, and my sufferings may manure the soil of the future harmony for somebody else. I want to see with my own eyes the hind lie down with the lion and the victim rise up and embrace his murderer. I want to be there when everyone suddenly understands what it has all been for. All the religions of the world are built on this longing, and I am a believer.[11]

Why is Ulrich's silence in the face of the world better than Arnheim's widely dispersed articulateness? Why does the search for unity lead the better man to withdraw from the world and the worse man to act upon it? The backgrounds of these questions lie close to the nature of modern literature. Let us take Melville's *Moby-Dick* as a point of departure. In this novel there are three major forces: the whale, Captain Ahab, and Ishmael. Let us say that these three forces roughly represent the irrational, inscrutable problem of life (the whale), human presumption in setting itself up as equal to this problem (Ahab), and the thinker who observes both as he is drawn along by the power of this presumption (Ishmael). If we look at serious fiction of the twentieth century, is it not striking how the Ishmael-figures dominate the scene and how the Ahabs have shrunk to secondary importance? What is Naphtha to Hans Castorp in Thomas Mann's *The Magic Mountain?* What is Arnheim to Ulrich? Even without Ahabs, modern literature is dominated by Ishmaels, the Blooms and the Zhivagos, the K.'s and the Castorps. Although these figures are passive, although it is life that challenges them rather than the other way around, they are the moral centers of the works, of the worlds, in which they appear.

Ulrich is passive in the world's sense, but in his own sense he has a fervent mission, which is to lay the groundwork for the future perfectibility of man. This is the base of the utopian note in *The Man without Qualities,* a note that is quite strong at the beginning but fades progressively as Ulrich fails to find any response to his ideals in the people around him. As this note fades, it is absorbed by the world of myth, specifically the myth of Isis and Osiris—as Musil presents it, the myth of the brother and sister who withdraw from the world and who, through an incestuous and mystic relationship, achieve a tenuous and temporary identity and unity denied them in the cosmopolitan world of the twentieth century. But are not myths also a kind of utopia? Do they not also, like a political utopia, present a world of stable relationships, or at least of stable cyclical process?

Is not, most importantly, the world of myth a closed world complete within itself?

I would like to argue that Musil came to the realization that the purely rational utopia he envisioned early in *The Man without Qualities* (Book I, Chapters 61 and 62) was too narrow, too much an artificial construction of thought. During the years he was working on the novel Musil seems to have moved more and more toward myth and mysticism as offering the only possible context for his utopian vision. The entire tone of the novel changes as it proceeds; if it starts out in the tone of Dean Swift it ends in that of William Blake. The mystic ecstasy of the third part of Musil's novel is in a different world from the cool intellectuality of the first part, and this other world is that of Blake's *Jerusalem:* "Go on, builders, in hope, tho' Jerusalem wanders far away / Without the gate of Los, among the dark Satanic wheels."

But whether in the realm of intellect or myth, the utopian *idea* is basic in *The Man without Qualities.* Musil once wrote that art is a partial realization of what ought to be, and he devoted his life to working out such a realization. The key to the utopian idea in Musil's second novel is already present in his first, *The Confusions of Young Törless.* It is to be found, I think, in Törless' emotional preoccupation with the problem of irrational numbers in mathematics which has already been touched upon. For Törless the problem is the leap from solid numbers to solid numbers over the bridge of irrational numbers, that is, numbers which do not exist. "Isn't it like a bridge of which only the two piers are there, and which one yet strides over as confidently as if it were all there?" [12] This kind of reckoning, Törless says, makes his head swim. Is it an accident that Musil once described *The Man without Qualities* as a bridge being built out into space? The image is suggestive: the one existing pier from which the bridge is being constructed would represent existing reality; the other pier, somewhere out there, would be the utopian solution; and the bridge itself, being built step by step toward the second pier, is Musil's novel, covering the span between where man is and where he ought to be.

The Man without Qualities was the work of a creative lifetime. This is evident in its unhurried scope, which dwarfs other attempts to deal with similar themes, attempts as ambitious as Hermann Broch's trilogy *The Sleepwalkers*. It is evident also in the way in which the human problems of the novel grow organically out of Musil's earlier works. Musil wrote in a sketch for an "Afterword" to *The Man without Qualities:*

> The book that I am now writing reaches with its beginnings almost, if not quite, back to the time I was writing my first book [*The Confusions of Young Törless*, published in 1906]. It ought to have become my second book. But I had at that time the correct feeling that I was not yet ready for it. An attempt I made to write the story of three people, in which Walter, Clarisse and Ulrich are clearly prefigured, ended after several hundred pages in nothing.[13]

Musil's diaries show the persistent presence of this work in his thought, although it does not come clearly to the fore until after the First World War. The war seems to have brought about a change of emphasis in the novel. Before the war human problems predominate in Musil's notes while the enormous historical, political, and social fabric of the work—which may have previously been present in Musil's mind—finds expression in his diaries only from the early 1920's. The novel was called at various times *The Savior* and *The Spy*, and its chief character was "Achilles," "Robert," and "Anders" (a German proper name meaning "different") before becoming "Ulrich." [14]

Seldom has a work of literature had such a long period of gestation, reaching in its totality almost forty years, and seldom has a work of literature been undertaken on so ambitious a scale. The novel as we have it in the Rowohlt edition, over 1,600 pages of small print on India paper, is only about half of what was to have been the eventual whole.[15] Musil, who had effectively withdrawn from the world after 1924 to devote himself exclusively to this one task, would suffer no interruption but the final one. The work he left behind upon his sudden death in 1942 at the age of sixty-two was not only unfinished, but, it seems to me, unfinishable. There is no neat scheme waiting to be rounded off, no clear development unfortunately interrupted. There is rather in the unfinished fragments an almost hunted uncertainty and confusion, a sense of lost direction and loss of purpose.

This is not meant as a negative criticism, for *The Man without Qualities* is clearly and consciously an attempt by Musil to objectify his thinking and the psychological background of his thinking. The power of the work is the power of this thought, and where the thought falters—due not to loss of vitality but to the realization that there are problems beyond its reach—the novel falters with it. The proof of the searching power of the work lies in its haunting quality; it is difficult to read but impossible to forget. Musil has succeeded in touching some basic chord of human life, and whatever his shortcomings he clearly belongs in the very front rank of twentieth-century artists.

Before turning to a more specific examination of selected aspects of *The Man without Qualities*, I would like to correct an aberration in critical perspective. The idea has got abroad that Musil is comparable to Joyce and Proust.[16] Such a comparison, it seems to me, can be valid only in the sense that the major efforts of all three belong in the category of the encyclopedic novel, as indicated at the beginning of this chapter. How to compare Musil and Proust? It is true that both deal with the decline and fall of a social order, but this resemblance is rather superficial. Proust is concerned with aesthetics, the aristocracy, and death, all under the spell of time. For Musil these elements are secondary; and while both authors share a deep interest in psychology, the emphases are so totally different that almost any comparison between them seems irrelevant. As for Joyce, Musil himself offers a sharp profile in a late collection of aphorisms. Joyce's work, he says, is

> Naturalism spiritualized.—A step that was mature even in 1900. His punctuation is naturalistic. With this also goes "indeceny." Attraction: How does a man live in cross-section? Compared to this I practice a heroic conception of art. Question: How does one think? His abbreviations are: short formulas for linguistically orthodox forms. They copy the . . . speech-process. Not the thinking process.[17]

If comparing Musil with Proust and Joyce sheds very little light on any of the three, comparing Musil with Mann and Tolstoy may shed much more on all. *The Magic Mountain* shares with *The Man without Qualities* a broad approach to the problems of life in modern Europe, the removal of its central figure from the main stream of the world for a period to get his bearings, and the use of an impending world war as a "thunderclap" which gives the action of both novels irony and urgency. Mann and Musil are farthest apart in the area of psychology, and here they are so far apart that I think a meaningful comparison of the two works must be limited to the thematic level.

A comparison of *The Man without Qualities* and *War and Peace* offers substance for fruitful reflection. Apart from some superficial resemblances this comparison can, I think, be reduced to two important points: both novels contain essentially the same view of history, although arrived at from different points of view, and both use the element of time in roughly the same way. The view of history, briefly stated, is that the "causes" of an act are so numerous that the human mind is incapable of encompassing the multitude of factors that lead to a given act. While Musil's microscope is focused on the psychological factors and Tolstoy's is largely focused on the chain-of-event factors, both are concerned with the problem of the irrational energy of an age and a country at a moment of historical crisis. In its treatment of time *The Man without Qualities* resembles the historical aspect of *War and Peace* and dissociates itself further from *Remembrance of Things Past* and *Ulysses*. For Tolstoy the historian, time is leading on in the direction of an ultimate, obscure destiny. For Musil the historian, time is leading on in the direction of an ultimate better life, although the immediate end is, ironically, war. For these writers time itself is the historical process, of which they are the observers: unlike Proust they are not interested in "conquering" time; unlike Joyce it means more to them than the mechanical unrolling of hours of day and night.

In Musil this attitude toward time is especially marked. One of the most important aspects of *The Man without*

Qualities is the ruthless subordination of chronological time, the succession of hours by the clock. One is only vaguely conscious of this clock time through occasional references to the season or the weather. The reader is caught up in a liquid flow that is not broken up into the neat little drips of the faucet of narrative time, of "then . . . and then . . . and then." In this careful minimizing of chronological time I see the chief cause of the reader's impression that both the actions and the characters of this novel are "undramatic." Taken individually both action and character in this novel are very skillfully done from the dramatic point of view, but in context, surrounded as they are by hundreds of more or less formal essays, they seem flat. Ulrich's confrontation with Arnheim, Moosbrugger's second murder, Clarisse's struggles with Walter are all compelling; but the dramatic impact of these incidents, because of the unusual way in which they are presented, is missed.

This procedure was quite deliberate on Musil's part; he has Ulrich himself explain in an essay the principle by which chronological time in the novel is subordinated, when the idea occurs to him that

> the law of this life, for which one yearns, . . . was none other than that of *narrative order*. This is the simple order that consists in one's being able to say: 'When that had happened, then this happened.' What puts our minds at rest is the simple sequence, the overwhelming variegation of life now represented in, as a mathematician would say, a unidimensional order: the stringing upon one thread of all that has happened in space and time, in short, that notorious 'narrative thread' of which it then turns out the thread of life itself consists. Lucky the man who can say 'when,' 'before' and 'after'! Misfortunes may have

befallen him, or he may have writhed in agony: but as soon as he is capable of recounting the events in their chronological order he feels as well content as if the sun were shining straight on his diaphragm. This is the thing that the novel has artificially turned to account: . . . something it would be hard to understand if this everlasting epic device, by means of which even nannies soothe their little charges, this tried and tested 'intellectual foreshortening,' this 'perspective of the mind,' were not part and parcel of life itself. In their basic relation to themselves most people are narrators. They do not like the lyrical, or at best they like it only for moments at a time. And even if a little 'because' and 'in order that' may get knotted into the thread of life, still, they abhor all cogitation that reaches out beyond that. What they like is the orderly sequence of facts, because it has the look of a necessity, and by means of the impression that their life has a 'course' they manage to feel somehow sheltered in the midst of chaos. And now Ulrich observed that he seemed to have lost this elementary narrative element to which private life still holds fast, although in public life everything has now become non-narrative, no longer following a 'thread,' but spreading out as an infinitely interwoven surface.[18]

In the following section I would like to indicate more specifically the structure and method of the novel, the various expressions of its theme, and the important characteristics of its characters; and, following this, to examine in some detail important and representative characters.

II

The Man without Qualities was intended to be a symmetrical structure in four parts. The "Sort of Introduction" was to have been balanced by a "Sort of Conclusion"; the long second part, "The Like of It Now Happens," which concerns the complex of problems surrounding the "Collateral Campaign" (*Parallelaktion*), was to have been balanced by the long third part, "Into the Millennium," or "The Criminals," which concerns the complex of problems surrounding the relationship of Ulrich and his sister Agathe.[19] Musil was only part way through the third part when he died, leaving for the rest of the novel an embarrassment of sketches, notes, early drafts, and outlines. The editor of the Rowohlt edition seems to have added to the confusion by a capricious ordering of these fragments. To point out the fourfold plan of the novel is to correct a foreshortening of critical perspective, for most of those who have written on *The Man without Qualities* have taken the action of the "Collateral Campaign" in the second part to be the central device of the novel. But it is hardly mentioned in the third part, which rises to the level of myth. The only continuity among the three parts of the novel we have is that of four figures: Ulrich, his friends Clarisse and Walter, and the murderer Moosbrugger. The other characters are confined to one of the three sections actually written.

I would like to advance the argument that the most helpful way of approaching this novel is to regard the third and the projected fourth parts as attempts to find a solution to the problems stated in the first part and elaborated in the second. A discussion of the most important of these problems will help provide a perspective for the understanding of the characters of this novel. For the culmination of *The Man without Qualities*, like that of every other novel, is in its characters; the values with which Musil approaches life, and which he ascribes to it, are ultimately contained in the carefully arranged lives of his characters.

These problems might best be compared to the weights at the two ends of a seesaw: as a sense of identity (denoting integrity, unity, and participation) falls in the national, social, and personal consciousness, a sense of possibility on these three levels correspondingly rises. In an age in which the sense of identity has been lost the cultured man finds nothing but possibilities to lean on, and as these are rather insubstantial supports such a man has all he can do to keep from falling down. The search through uncertain possibilities for a firm support of belief is, in a sentence, what *The Man without Qualities* is about. The early part of the twentieth century was such a period of loss of the sense of identity, a loss which Hermann Broch has summed up in *The Sleepwalkers:* "Amid a blurring of all forms, in a twilight of apathetic uncertainty brooding over a ghostly world, man like a lost child gropes his way by the help of a small frail thread of logic through a dream landscape that he calls reality and that is nothing but a nightmare to him." [20] Chapter 16 of *The Man without Qualities*, titled "A mysterious disease of the times," presents the argument that although modern society has progressed materially something intangible, an illusion or power of illusion, has been lost. Ulrich

imagined that the great churchman and philosopher, Thomas Aquinas (*ob.* 1274), after having, by unspeakable exertions, got the ideas of his time arranged in the most orderly system possible, had gone still further down to the bottom of it all and had only just finished; and now, having by special grace remained young, he stepped out of his round-arched doorway, a pile of folios under his arm, and an electric tram shot right past in front of him. The uncomprehending amazement of the *doctor universalis*, as the past had called the celebrated Thomas, amused him.[21]

We might first look at the lighter end of the seesaw, at what I have called the decline of identity. Here we see, on the three levels referred to above, a variety of forms which have lost their content. On the national and social levels the empire and the city, and on the personal level the family, the career, and the private life, are seen as shells of what they used to be. Like an old car Austria-Hungary moves along on sheer momentum, held together not by any bonds of inner unity but merely by habit and habitual tension. The Modern City (Vienna) is presented impressionistically with great skill in the opening chapter of the work; little dabs of suggested color and sound convey an impression of the cacophonous multiplicity of urban life—an impression consisting of individual details, not a harmonious whole. Musil emphasizes that the city is important not for its uniqueness but for its "cityness," and the impersonality of the city as he presents it is quite remarkable. It is also most important that this is a city of man, not of God, and is a reflection of the disunity of man's life rather than the perfection of a divine order.

In his presentation of the city Musil lays special emphasis on its lack of style. Style might be roughly defined here as a sense of total meaning; the components of a house, or an empire, or a man's life have style only when they form a harmonious whole. The "little castle" that Ulrich rents has been put together haphazardly at various periods; it is a conglomeration of separate styles which has no style as a whole. (The early twentieth century's lack of a style of its own, for which it substituted frantic imitation of styles from other periods, is one of the major themes of Broch's *The Sleepwalkers.*)

What we have in *The Man without Qualities,* on many levels, are components without a pattern. On the national and social levels the sense of identity has been lost; filling up the vacuum left by this loss is a peculiar energy that has no specific direction, but erupts in a great variety of ambiguous forces. From the sterile spirit that reigned in Europe from 1880 to 1900, Musil tells us, a fever arose all over the continent; everyone felt that something was fermenting, but no one knew whether it would take the form of a new art, a new morality, or social upheaval. This feeling led to all sorts of experimentation, he continues, much of it eccentric. Musil sums up this period as "a small rebirth and Reformation."[22] This energy is, of course, to erupt in war, which is the ultimate expression of irrational energy. In connection with this force, which runs through the novel like an underground chain of fungi, one of the most important problems of the book must be mentioned: the problem of irrationality.

As a mathematician and a man of intellect, Ulrich in his search for new and better values operates on the plane of reason, at least until he flees with his sister Agathe into the realm of myth. But like mushrooms popping up from some underground network little outbursts of purely irrational violence keep pushing up into Ulrich's rational world. Three such incidents occur in the introductory part of the novel, the first of these on the second page. A man is hit by a truck; a crowd gathers around him as he lies on the sidewalk. A couple makes comments on the accident, and an ambulance arrives. The blind irrationality of this by-product of modern urban life is emphasized by the studiously neutral tone and the factual, impersonal description which Musil gives of the scene. The lady of the couple does not feel easy about this sudden violence until her escort offers statistics on traffic accidents. This desire to fit everything into a pattern, to subsume the irrational in a rational order, however tenuous, is one of the major themes of *The Man without Qualities*. It is a defense mechanism; the resulting impersonality of the rationalization is felt by the characters involved as removing something which threatens their existence.

Musil indicates the tenuousness of this rationalizing process, and perhaps better than any other novelist conveys a stark impression of the chaotic abyss, the empty nothingness, which man tries to cover over with a thin floor of talk and intellectual rationalization. The traffic accident, Ulrich's random blow at the punching bag in his dressing room after he has been reflecting on the undirected energy of the time, or the incident in which he is beaten up and robbed on the street one night are typical small examples of the presence of irrational force. A much larger example is the severe mental depression which overcomes Ulrich at critical moments in the novel when he realizes the failure of his attempts to explain life rationally; these moments of crisis will be touched on later. The problem of the sex-murderer Moosbrugger is also, I think, to be understood in connection with this problem of irrationality. Part of Ulrich's fascination by the Moosbrugger case arises from the discrepancy between the placid carpenter himself and the violence of his deeds.

This half-hidden conflict in *The Man without Qualities* between the monstrosity of irrational force and man's attempt to overcome it by the use of reason seems to me to account for the extreme tension evident throughout the novel. The same tension underlies *The Confusions of Young Törless*, *The Visionaries*, and stories such as "Grigia" and "The Portuguese Lady." This is the quality which gives urgency to Ulrich's search for new moral values; behind his search is the conviction that, if these values are not found and thrown up as a dike, everything that man has created will be swept away.

The decline of identity is perhaps more urgent on the personal level than it is on the national and social levels. Within a dissolving social context that has no central core the individual can no longer build his life around an integral set of values. This is Ulrich's problem, and it is why he is the central character of *The Man without Qualities*. This problem infects every area of his life: his family relationships, his careers, his relationships with his friends, and even his sex life.

We are first told about the background of this man without qualities in an excursive manner that is rather too familiar to readers of traditional German novels, and indeed might be taken as a parody of them. The starting point in the present of *The Man without Qualities* is seen as the result of a long chain of past experiences, the culmination of which is a frosty politeness between Ulrich's sixty-nine-year-old father and the thirty-two-year-old son—an estrangement which arises from a conflict between the father's values and those of the son. The title of the chapter in which this estrangement is presented is "Even a Man Without Qualities has a father with qualities,"[23] and in spite of the son's irritation at the father's eighteenth-century courtly respect for order, position, and social obligation Ulrich is very much his father's son.

The son's dissociation from the father and his lack of contact with his sister Agathe, who is first mentioned in a letter from the father at the very end of the introductory section of the novel, indicate the decayed state of the family ties. The sense of identity, even in this most basic human group, is absent. But Ulrich owes a great deal to his father, not least to his relative wealth and to his position as a member of the lower aristocracy which give Ulrich the independence and social status indispensable to being a man without qualities. Relieved of the responsibilities of earning a living, he can be the purely contemplative man, reflecting even in his attempts at activity the loss of identity in the world he lives in.

This is not to say that Ulrich is indolent or incompetent, for he has run through three careers, as a soldier, as an engineer, and as a mathematician, and at least in the last field has earned the respect of experts for his work. But there is something lacking *in Ulrich* which cannot be imputed—at least directly—to the time, something that prevents him from committing himself seriously to any of these endeavors. There is also something lacking in all the people surrounding Ulrich. The women he attracts, principally his successive mistresses, are pathetically incomplete. The first of these, Leona, is a glutton, the second, "Bonadea," a nymphomaniac. Nor are Ulrich's childhood friends, the petulant dilettante Walter and his wife Clarisse (who is neurotic at the beginning of the novel and insane by the time it breaks off), superior specimens of humanity. All the individuals attracted to Ulrich, culminating with his sister Agathe, are in important respects human wrecks drawn by some mysterious current onto Ulrich's shore. It is in my opinion quite doubtful whether these wrecks were caused by any disease of the times; Musil was not simplistic in his approach to character, and as a trained psychologist he seems to prefer to present his figures as suffering from innate defects. There is no doubt, however, that these defects are revealed and aggravated by the peculiar conditions of the age, in much the same way as Thomas Mann emphasizes in *The Magic Mountain* that a disease latent under ordinary conditions will spring to life in the cold thin air of the magic mountain.

This loss of personal identity, then, and the simultaneous loss of national and social identity, form a basic problem of *The Man without Qualities*. Musil believes that the way to regain these identities and achieve unity is straight through the most unsettling aspect of this unjointed world—through possibility. This idea, as Ulrich sees it, has much in common with Kleist's curious notion (in his essay "On the Marionette Theater") that in order to re-enter the Garden of Eden man must go around the earth and get in the back way.

We now find ourselves at the other end of our hypothetical seesaw, the down end; and the principle of possibility which occupies this dominant position may be called the central principle of *The Man without Qualities*. It occupies this position because of the times; in an age in which identity is no problem possibility as a basic principle of life would be irrelevant. If Ulrich had been involved in the Crusades, it is doubtful if he would have thought of Mohammedanism as an alternative possibility to Christianity.

Musil's conception of possibility is clearly explained near the beginning of the novel—*before* we have been introduced to the central character—in Book I, Chapter 4, which is entitled "If there is such a thing as a sense of reality, there must also be a sense of possibility."[24] In this chapter Musil presents a systematic defense of a "sense of possibility," which he sees as parallel to a "sense of reality." Possibility is intimately connected with a lack of qualities. Anyone who has this sense of possibility

> does not say, for instance: Here this or that has happened, will happen, must happen. He uses his imagination and says: Here such and such might, should or ought to happen. And if he is told that something *is* the way it is, then he thinks: Well, it could probably just as easily be some other way. So the sense of possibility might be defined outright as the capacity to think how everything could 'just as easily' be, and to attach no more importance to what is than to what is not. It will be seen that the consequences of such a creative disposition may be remarkable, and unfortunately they not infrequently make the things that other people admire appear wrong and the things that other people prohibit permissible, or even make both appear a matter of indifference. Such possibilitarians live, it is said, within a finer web, a web of haze, imaginings, fantasy and the subjunctive mood.[25]

This sense, which finds expression as an attitude of mind, is thus essentially negative, and as it removes both value and purpose from reality it is also paralytic, at least from the point of view of the "other people." Implied in Musil's definition is the idea that the possibilitarian must be detached from things and place himself in the position of an observer in relation to them; seeing possibilities is a reflective, not an active process.

It is important, however, that acceptance of possibility does not destroy reality; Musil's conception of possibility is as an *alternative* real action. He states:

It is reality that awakens possibilities, and nothing could be more wrong than to deny this. Nevertheless, in the sum total or on the average they will always remain the same possibilities, going on repeating themselves until someone comes along to whom something real means no more than something imagined. It is he who first gives the new possibilities their meaning and their destiny; he awakens them.[26]

This last sentence contains, it seems to me, a key to the third part of the novel, "Into the Millennium," for in an ultimate sense Musil thinks that possibilities *have* meaning and destinies. Ulrich's "expedition" in the mythical and almost mystical third part of *The Man without Qualities* may be seen as an attempt to turn possibility into a final reality. He fails. But as Musil points out in the early chapter on possibility, the possibilitarian is no superman:

Such a man is, however, by no means an unambiguous matter. Since his ideas, in so far as they are not mere idle phantasmagoria, are nothing else than as yet unborn realities, he too of course has a sense of reality; but it is a sense of possible reality and moves towards its goal much more slowly than most people's sense of their real possibilities. He wants, as it were, the wood, and the others the trees; and the wood in itself is something that is very difficult to express, whereas trees mean so and so many cubic feet of a definite quality. Or perhaps it can be put better by saying that the man with an ordinary sense of reality resembles a fish that nibbles at the hook and does not see the line, while the man with the kind of sense of reality that one can also call the sense of possibility pulls a line through the water without any notion whether there is a bait on it or not. In him an extraordinary indifference to the life nibbling at the bait is in contrast with the probability that he will do utterly eccentric things.[27]

In a preface to *An Evening with Mr. Teste* Paul Valéry writes about the French counterpart to Musil's Ulrich that Mr. Teste "is impossible, for he is nothing other than the very demon of possibility. He is dominated by anxiety about the totality of what he could do. . . . He knows only two values, two categories, which are those of the consciousness reduced to its acts, the possible and the impossible."[28]

In a world without fixed boundaries either outside the human mind or within it, Musil's argument runs, the man who wants to accomplish something in life will (paradoxically) stand back from life and choose the least direct way of arriving at his goal, through the realm of possibility. The final sentence of this chapter sums up the theme and prepares the reader for the introduction in the following chapter of the novel's major figure:

> And since the possession of qualities presupposes that one takes a certain pleasure in their reality, all this gives us a glimpse of how it may all of a sudden happen to someone who cannot summon up any sense of reality—even in relation to himself—that one day he appears to himself as a man without qualities.[29]

"*To himself*"—the possibilitarian has been set up as a type, but is now to be seen as an individual.

The sense of possibility saturates not only the central figure of *The Man without Qualities* but also the novel as a whole. The man without qualities is presented as living in a world of "qualities without man"; and this is evident in the neuroses and separation from reality which afflict, in varying degrees, all but a few of the novel's characters. But again, Musil has made a virtue of possibility; he advocates the radical method of regaining a real sense of identity by withdrawing from active participation in life and embracing the sense of possibility.

A summary of the progression of the two larger divisions of *The Man without Qualities*, followed by a discussion of important aspects of the novel's method, will complete the background against which individual characters will be examined. Most of the articles which have so far appeared on Musil's giant work are concerned almost exclusively with the second part, specifically with the social and political themes there woven together in the "Collateral Campaign," the committee organized to explore ways to celebrate the seventieth jubilee of Franz Josef in 1918 as a counter to plans by the upstart Prussians to celebrate the thirtieth jubilee of Wilhelm II in the same year. This focusing of critical perspective on one aspect of the novel is as much a mistake as singling out the Gretchen story in Goethe's *Faust* as the central part of that work; and it leads to the same kind of distortion. For like *Faust*, *The Man without Qualities* moves from the world of reality to the world of myth, although the two are not as far apart in Musil's novel as in Goethe's drama; the "reality" of the second part of *The Man without Qualities*, as seen through Ulrich's eyes, is tinged with Fichtean subjectivism. Its realness is a relative quality, dependent on the state of mind of the observer. The "myth" of the third part, on the other hand, takes place in the real world, and is subject to social tensions and pressures. Musil describes this myth-process as

> a voyage on the edge of the possible. . . . [Ulrich] and Agathe came upon a road that had something to do with the occupation of the God-seized, but they walked this road without being pious, without believing in God or soul, indeed without even believing in a Beyond and an afterlife; they had come

upon this road as people of this world, and walked it as such: and precisely this was what was noteworthy about it.[30]

The second and third parts of the novel are close in another respect. Both present separate attempts by Ulrich, in different spheres, to find a unity in life, and both attempts fail. Near the end of the second part Ulrich makes a supreme effort to turn the Collateral Campaign into an instrument for the achievement of utopia. From some obscure feeling within him he bursts out with the following passionate speech to Count Leinsdorf, chairman of the committee:

> There is but one single task for the Collateral Campaign: to form the beginning of a spiritual general inventory! We must do approximately what would be necessary if the Day of Judgment was to fall in the year 1918, and the old spirit was to be cut off and a higher one to begin. Found in the name of His Majesty a Global Secretariat of Exactitude and Soul; all other tasks before that one are insoluble or merely illusory! [31]

In the final chapters of this part Ulrich realizes the hopelessness of this task and in a mood of despondency withdraws from it. The death of his father provides him with an excuse to leave the world of Viennese society and the Collateral Campaign, which ceases to be an important factor in the novel. His year's leave almost half gone, Ulrich feels at the end of the second part that he has accomplished nothing. His reacquaintance with his sister Agathe, who is almost a complete stranger to him, is the basis for the third part of the work, "Into the Millennium" or "The Criminals."

While the second part of *The Man without Qualities* is oriented around urban, social, political, and historical themes, the third part is oriented around moral, ethical, and mythical ones. Like everything else in the period these two sets of values have lost their connection with each other; Ulrich's ethically motivated call for a "spiritual general inventory," directed at the socially and politically motivated Collateral Campaign, falls on deaf ears. Both these sets of values will be brought out in greater detail in discussion of the characters. For the moment I would like to emphasize the element of myth, which is the most difficult.

The myth used by Musil in his novel is explicitly that of Isis and Osiris, the brother and sister who find completion in each other (in 1923 the *Neue Rundschau* published a hyper-Freudian poem by Musil called "Isis and Osiris" [32]). This myth has affinities with the androgynous concept of love mentioned in Plato's *Symposium.* The psychological implications of the myth are explored at great length by Musil in both novel and poem. But the larger significance of this particular myth for *The Man without Qualities* lies in its element of two separate parts which are the same part, which form a harmonious unity together, which belong together. This myth thus applies not only to Ulrich and Agathe, but to all the spheres of the novel: man and family, man and society, man and self. Ulrich and his sister attempt to realize the myth of Isis and Osiris literally in the modern world, to use it as a means of forming a whole out of their partial lives. It is this attempt to realize the myth literally which gives rise to the moral and ethical problems, which are anything but conventional, in the third part of the work.

Myth has become very popular with writers and critics in the twentieth century. It is therefore important to make clear how different authors regard it. "A contemporary myth," Musil noted in his diary around 1931 in discussing his Isis-Osiris poem and its relation to his novel, "contains intellectual elements. It contains a 'partial solution.' A myth must be believe-able [*glaub-würdig*]. Only today it isn't completely believed. Was it ever? Apparently not. It will always have been something half-believed, for in complete gods- and demons-faiths men would not have been able to live at all as practically as they always did." [33]

In this attitude toward myth as a part of the real world Musil differs from the Joyce of *Ulysses* and *Finnegans Wake* and the Mann of the *Joseph* novels and *The Holy Sinner*. In Joyce's large novels myth is present largely as a sophisticated construction on the part of the author, while in Mann's works irony is used to keep myth always in the realm of "play," in Schiller's sense. But Ulrich and Agathe in *The Man without Qualities* are serious in trying *consciously* to realize the myth for the sake of new values which they feel it represents. Here it is not framework but substance. In this Musil's conception of myth is similar to that of Blake, and, as I have suggested above, it can be most illuminating to think of myth in Musil's novel in Blakean terms. Musil made it quite clear that for him the center of his novel lay in its mythical rather than its social aspect. In the same diary entry quoted above he wrote: "Reminded of *Isis-Osiris* poem. It contains the novel in nucleus. The novel has been reproached with perversity: rebuttal: the archaic and the schizophrenic express themselves artistically harmoniously, yet they are totally different. Just so can the brother-sister feeling be perverse and it can be myth." [34]

If *The Man without Qualities* culminated in myth, or in the achievement by Ulrich and Agathe of a mythical state, the effect of the entire novel would have been one thing. But there is a way out of as well as a way into the millennium, and the failure of brother and sister to achieve their aim radically alters the effect of the work. In the fragmentary third part of the novel Ulrich and Agathe withdraw from Vienna to an island in the Adriatic where they consummate their mystically prepared incest. The tone of ecstasy, quite unlike the tone of sharp irony in the first and second parts, rises to an incredible pitch; the language, while still keeping its precision, casts a shimmering image of the setting and of the peculiar couple called in an earlier chapter heading "The constellation of the siblings, or the unseparated and not united." [35] But Ulrich and Agathe admit to themselves the failure of their attempt to find an entry to paradise. What follows is unclear; Agathe drops out of the novel, perhaps to commit suicide (although she is mentioned in other fragments as being alive during the war), and Ulrich returns to Vienna.

It is impossible to know what Musil would have done with his characters after this experience; the uncertainty evident in his notes and sketches makes one wonder whether he knew himself. *The Man without Qualities* is more than most books one which the author worked out as he wrote; when a book is written over such a long span of years, it is natural that the author's intentions may slowly change; *Faust* is the modern archetype of this situation. Therefore it is futile to speculate how Musil might have finished his novel; more interesting is the question *whether* he could have finished it. It is said of Gertrude Stein that before she died she asked: "What is the answer?" and when no answer came asked: "In that case, what is the question?" It seems to me that in the fascinating fragment of this third part Musil was moving from the first of these questions to the second.

At all events, Musil suggests that the answer to the problem of life in the twentieth century is not to be found on a permanent basis by a flight into myth. But this failure, like the others, seems to be an attempt by Ulrich to do what Ulrich cannot do, that is to realize himself a utopia that at best will be realized by future generations, if at all. He himself, as has been previously noted, described his generation as on an expedition the fruits of which would be realized by posterity. This conflict between Ulrich as representative of the modern man of intellect and Ulrich as an individual with personal problems is only to be explained by a gradual change in Musil's attitude toward his major character and toward his novel.

This change might be called a growing inward; in the first and second parts of the work Ulrich is presented largely from the outside, and the reader has the clear impression that the author is building an objective character through whom to present his ideas. This is the Ulrich who envisions a future utopia and who is terribly concerned about setting up a secretariat of exactitude and soul. But the Ulrich of the third part of the novel is different from this; here we find an Ulrich who is terribly concerned about himself and about finding his own right place in the world. He takes on an urgency which is deeper and more compelling.

To turn to more concrete matters, an indication of some important aspects of the novel's method might help the reader to gain a clearer understanding of the work. It has already been shown that Musil's rejection of narrative order was deliberate; his aim was to present an impression of unreality in a real world. "I want a picture of the world," he wrote in his diary around 1919 or 1920, "the real background, in order to unfold my unreality in front of it. I observe life since 1880, the determining period for people between 20 and 60." [36] Correspondingly one finds in *The Man without Qualities* that physical settings are often described in precise detail, while the personages—their appearance, gestures—rarely are, a characteristic which has been mentioned in connection with Musil's earlier works. What is described about the characters are their ideas, their feelings, and their states of mind; the "action" is frequently stopped like a single frame in a movie film while the flux of a character's mind during a single instant is described and analyzed. This of course slows down the tempo of the work.

Generally speaking one might say that in this novel description replaces narration. Also, the proportion of nondialogue to dialogue is very high, and much of the metaphysically abstract dialogue is such only by virtue of the quotation marks surrounding it, while a great deal of the nondialogue consists of the reporting of the substance of conversations. It must be remembered that this technique was highly deliberate (although in the unpruned third part of the work it certainly got out of hand). Speaking of a commercially successful book, Musil wrote about a passage he had just quoted: "If I were to accustom myself to this a little I could write such places too. . . . But I don't want to. Any talented person can carry on this tradition. And thus I have preferred to try the unenjoyable. Someone must sometime tie a knot in this infinite thread." [37] This statement might sound like a rationalization, but nowhere does Musil apologize for his radical approach to literature.

Certainly the most important single aspect of the style of *The Man without Qualities* apart from the brilliant use of language (one critic has described Musil's language as "a utopian mixture of precision, passion and irony" [38]) is what Musil calls "essayism." The novel itself contains not only frequent and extensive commentaries by the author which have no direct connection with the "story," but also a formal justification of the procedure itself (Book I, Chapter 62). Essayism is presented as the principle according to which Ulrich's mind works:

There was something in Ulrich's nature that worked in a haphazard, paralysing, disarming manner against logical systematization, against the one-track will, against the definitely directed urges of ambition; and it was also connected with his chosen expression, 'Essayism,' even although this something in him contained precisely those elements that he had, in the course of time and with unconscious care, eliminated from that concept. The translation of the word 'essay' as 'attempt,' which is the generally accepted one, only approximately gives the most important allusion to the literary model. For an essay is not the provisional or incidental expression of a conviction that might on a more favourable occasion be elevated to the status of truth or that might just as easily be recognized as error (of that kind are only the articles and treatises, referred to as 'chips from their workshop,' with which learned persons favour us); an essay is the unique and unalterable form that a man's inner life assumes in a decisive thought. Nothing is more alien to it than that irresponsibility and semi-finishedness of mental images known as subjectivity; but neither are 'true' and 'false,' 'wise' and 'unwise,' terms that can be applied to such thoughts, which are nevertheless subject to laws that are no less strict than they appear to be delicate and ineffable. There have been quite a number of such essayists and masters of the floating life within, but there would be no point in naming them. Their domain lies between religion and knowledge, between example and doctrine, between *amor intellectualis* and poetry, they are saints with and without religion, and sometimes too they are simply men who have gone out on an adventure and lost their way.[39]

According to this description the essayist is an observer and a commentator who tries to look at the variety of life without judging it; the concept of "essayism" itself is, I think, another example of Musil's application of Mach's idea of functional relationships to that morality which is commonly judged by the absolute standards of " 'true' and 'false,' 'wise' and 'unwise.' " Another important point about essayism in *The Man without Qualities* is that, more than a device, it is an integral part of the fabric of the novel. A good example of this is the essay on essayism just quoted, which begins with a description of an attitude of Ulrich's and then shifts to a general commentary. This integration of the essay in Musil's novel may be contrasted with the essays in *War and Peace* or in the third part of Broch's trilogy *The Sleepwalkers*, which are presented in separate chapters and thus isolated from the narrative itself; or it may be contrasted with the essays in Musil's own first novel, *The Confusions of Young Törless*, in which essay and narrative never quite blend smoothly.

Essayism is, of course, nothing new. Basically it is an intrusion of an author directly into his work to explain, illuminate, comment on, or destroy the seriousness of what is going on. I would say that it generally arises from a feeling on the part of the author (unless he is simply trying to mock his subject matter) that a fictional vehicle is an inadequate means of presenting all that he is trying to say; that certain things he wants to express cannot be expressed through the form of his vehicle. Thus Fielding in *Tom Jones* put in separate chapters at the beginning of each part essays on the theory of literature which are not part of the novel. The innate relationship between essayism and irony is obvious. It is based squarely on the fact of the intrusion of the author into his work. The reasons for this intrusion, and indeed even the effects of it, are secondary. I would like to maintain that the very fact of intrusion sets up an ironic situation, whether or not it is developed as such. An author always enters his work in such a case as superior to the work and to the figures in the work. It is as if a puppetmaster were to put his arm down onto the stage with his puppets. The mere sight of the arm is enough to destroy the illusion of the audience that the puppets are acting in imitation of reality.

Musil's essayism is unlike that of Fielding and Broch, as I have indicated, in that it is an organic part of the novel. One important effect of this is to slow down and broaden the book; instead of an active picture of the drama of individual lives one has a reflective contemplation of an entire age. Thus in Musil's novel essayism serves at least partly the function of what Goethe and Schiller, in their correspondence on epic poetry, called a "retarding force," a force introduced to sustain suspense about the interrupted action and also to broaden the scope of the work.

This essayism is of course far from unique in literature. What is unique is Musil's conscious use of it as a basic structural element. His relation to society as author of *The Man without Qualities* is that of an essayist. An American reader is strongly tempted to think that Musil is a European Thoreau, and that if Thoreau had written a novel it would have been of the Musilian kind. Musil mentions Thoreau several times in his diaries; it is remarkable how closely they resemble each other in the tone in which they write about the world around them, although Thoreau is rustic compared to Musil. The following passage from *Cape Cod*, for instance, will surprise the reader of *The Man without Qualities:*

I have just heard of a Cape Cod captain who was expected home in the beginning of the winter from the West Indies, but was long since given up for lost, till his relations at length have heard with joy, that, after getting within forty miles of Cape Cod light, he was driven back by nine successive gales to Key West, between Florida and Cuba, and was once again shaping his course for home. Thus he spent his winter. In ancient times the adventures of these two or three men and boys would have been made the basis of a myth, but now such tales are crowded into a line of shorthand signs, like an algebraic formula, in the shipping news.[40]

The concept and functions of irony in *The Man without Qualities* are without doubt the most difficult part of the entire work. One cannot pretend to discuss the subject exhaustively in the course of a few pages, but it is most important to realize what it means to Musil and how he uses it in his novel. Basically Musil regards irony not as a device but as an intrinsic attitude toward life itself. Irony is at the heart of Musil's wide-ranging conception of "possibility" and the "possibilitarian"; to see things simultaneously as they are, and as they just as well could be but are not, is certainly an ironic attitude. And irony here has its basic function in *The Man without Qualities*, which is to dissolve the cement of relationships in the novel between one person and another and between people and the world they live in. Irony in this sense creates detachment, and in the case of Ulrich paralysis, for the possibilitarian, an ironic personality, cannot commit himself to any course of action. In another sense, as we have seen, irony is closely allied in this novel with essayism; this is the irony of the participation of the author in his work. And in yet another sense irony in

Musil's novel is closely connected with myth and the conception of utopia.

Irony is the way to myth and utopia, for only a person who is detached from life and able to weigh its possibilities in expectation of an ultimate ideal is aware of the value of myth and utopia. This is why, I think, there is in the third part of the novel an extensive discussion of faith in which St. Paul's description of it ("the substance of things hoped for, the evidence of things not seen") is referred to. A committed person, such as Arnheim, Agathe's husband Hagauer, General Stumm von Bordwehr, or even the criminal Moosbrugger, is by virtue of his commitment to everyday reality unable to conceive of either a mythical ritual or a utopian existence, or of the need for either. Through their commitment to the daily present these characters do not see the unreality of their own lives. Ulrich, freed from this commitment and seeking a new and better morality, leads his like-minded sister Agathe along the path of myth in the search for utopia. That they do not find it, or rather do not succeed in maintaining it, does not detract from the seriousness of the attempt. But such an attempt presupposes the ironic situation. I think this is the point that Northrop Frye is making in his *Anatomy of Criticism* when he writes that "irony . . . begins in realism and dispassionate observation. But as it does so, it moves steadily towards myth, and dim outlines of sacrificial rituals and dying gods begin to reappear in it. . . . This reappearance of myth in the ironic is particularly clear in Kafka and Joyce," [41] and, he might have added, in Musil.

Irony in the more conventional literary sense is also present in *The Man without Qualities.* There is, for instance, the irony of the time and setting of the novel. The Austrian

Empire is on the point of catastrophic war and dissolution, but most of the people in the work are blind to both; they muddle on as if their world was to go on forever. Musil uses the reader's knowledge of the approaching war to give an ironic effect to actions, statements and situations of the characters. The reader knows something important about them that they do not know themselves.

It has been indicated in earlier chapters that irony in its various senses was also present in Musil's earlier works. But in *The Man without Qualities* it has assumed a new dimension. Here it is not only a conscious tool used incidentally by the author, but also, in its more basic form, a part of the structure of the novel itself. Irony in *The Visionaries,* for instance, is used more for its dramatic than for its metaphysical value; in the novel this emphasis is reversed.

Irony, then, is a basic concept in the novel, but one should also keep in mind that it is used as a technique. This technique is based on what might be called the principle of incongruity. Musil states this principle in Book I, Chapter 49, of *The Man without Qualities:*

> Put a greyhound beside a pug-dog, a willow beside a poplar, a wine-glass on a freshly ploughed field, or a portrait into a sailing-boat instead of an art exhibition, in short, put side by side two highly bred and distinct forms of life, and what happens is that between them a void comes into existence, a mutual cancelling out, an utterly malicious absurdity with no bottom to it.[42]

Most of the immediate irony in the work derives from this principle. The incongruity of General Stumm in a library, or the contrast between Arnheim and his Moorish servant Soliman, or the difference between Moosbrugger's attitude toward the world and the attitude of the other characters toward him, are all cases in point. Some of the most powerful writing in the book is in elaboration of this principle, as when Musil writes:

By exercising great and manifold skill we manage to produce a dazzling deception by the aid of which we are capable of living alongside the most uncanny things and remaining perfectly calm about it, because we recognize these frozen grimaces of the universe as a table or a chair, a shout or an outstretched arm, a speed or a roast chicken. We are capable of living between one open chasm of the sky above our heads and one slightly camouflaged chasm of the sky beneath our feet, feeling ourselves as untroubled on the earth as in a room with the door locked. We know that life ebbs away both out into the inhuman distances of interstellar space and down into the inhuman construction of the atom-world; but in between there is a stratum of forms that we treat as the things that make up the world, without letting ourselves be in the least disturbed by the fact that this signifies nothing but a preference given to the sense-data received from a certain middle distance. . . . The most important intellectual devices produced by mankind serve the preservation of a constant state of mind, and all the emotions, all the passions in the world are a mere nothing compared to the vast but utterly unconscious effort that mankind makes in order to maintain its exalted peace of mind. It seems to be hardly worth while to speak of it, so perfectly does it function. But if one looks into it more closely one sees that it is nevertheless an extremely artificial state of mind that enables man to walk upright between the circling constellations and permits him, in the midst of the almost infinite *terra incognita* of the world around him, to place his hand with dignity between the second and third buttons of his coat.[43]

This passage, which illuminates Törless, Thomas, and Ulrich, also reveals the frustration which seems to underlie

The Man without Qualities. The selection is an attack upon man's complacency in the midst of an eternity in which he is completely accidental, but it does not offer a means by which man might reconcile himself with this eternity. Pascal too was frightened by the silence of space (as Musil apparently thought man should be), but went on to use it as an argument for the existence of God. Eliot, in *Four Quartets*, found a not dissimilar solution in religion: "Upon the sodden floor / Below, the boarhound and the boar / Pursue their pattern as before / But reconciled among the stars." Musil's approach to the problem from an intellectual point of view was perhaps not enough; for the intellect is, after all, a narrow base on which to reconcile into unity all the disparate fragments of modern life. The increasingly mystic quality of the third part of the novel, its emphasis on "soul" rather than "exactitude," perhaps indicates Musil's growing awareness of this fact. At any rate he took the irony described in the passage above very seriously indeed.

Two effects of irony are extremely important in this novel. One is the belittling of character by presenting the incongruity between a character's picture of himself and the picture of him seen by another character or by the author; the other is to effect a fragmentation of values by destroying the bonds of belief that make the world livable. Both these effects are negative. Musil is here following the procedure used by Nietzsche of a frontal assault on the blind acceptance by modern European man of the world as it is; Musil shares with Nietzsche the fateful flaw of becoming uncertain and vague in attempting to formulate new values to replace this blind acceptance. Irony, an admirable wrecking machine in the hands of a skilled operator, is not a good building machine.

In the course of writing *The Man without Qualities* Musil seems to have recognized this. At least, as the novel develops, conventional literary irony—the most obvious kind—progressively fades. In the first and second parts it is so pervasive, and one might add so lumbering, as almost to make the reader consider the work a satire. But in the third part this irony has yielded to the seriousness of Ulrich's (and Musil's) quest for a new morality and for the utopia of the "other condition." It has yielded to the basic ironic situation posited at the beginning of this discussion as the basis of Ulrich's quest.

In view of the lapse of time involved in the work's composition this change in the use of irony is hardly surprising; but this chronological factor should not blind us to the entirely different function of the third part of the work as opposed to the first two. In the first two Musil showed in great detail the bankruptcy of modern life; in the third he attempted to show, however hesitantly, the way to future redemption, a progression not unlike that in Eliot's *The Waste Land* from the "unreal city" to the key to salvation presumably offered by Eastern mysticism. Obviously irony cannot be used in the same way in presenting the bankruptcy of modern life and in indicating the way to future redemption; obviously it has a much greater scope in the former sphere and a much more limited one in the latter. But in both respects in *The Man without Qualities*, irony is basic to an understanding of the novel.

After this brief and necessarily incomplete discussion of irony in Musil's novel, an outline of the important general features of the characters in the work will help correlate what has gone before with a more detailed discussion of the individual protagonists. Musil's figures may be said to embody types of social attitudes. They are at the same time representative of the age and they *are* the age. The indecision of Ulrich, Clarisse's neurosis, and Arnheim's superficial success are qualities of the period. The occurrence of these qualities in these specific individuals is in this sense to be taken as a manifestation of a social sickness.

This double focus results in a problem of perspective in *The Man without Qualities:* Where is the dividing line between individuals as individuals and individuals as symbols of the time? Musil treats his characters with few exceptions —General Stumm is one—as case histories. In discussing Bonadea's nymphomania, for instance, Musil writes that "she was sensual as other people suffer from other ills, for example sweating or changing color easily. Apparently she had been born that way, and she could never prevail against it." [44] Especially in the first part of the novel one notices a lack of sympathy on the part of the author with many of his characters; he spits them on pins and examines them with clinical meticulousness. Ulrich's first mistress, the poor glutton Leona, is a prime example of this. This attitude of Musil's can be traced back, I think, to his belief that men and their attitudes are variations of recurrent types, and are chiefly interesting as such. One effect of this is that the reader does not care very much about the people portrayed; as he begins *The Man without Qualities* he finds that the life of the novel is in its ideas.

But as the work progresses, the major characters rise above this limiting tendency; they seem to get out of the author's control, and as they do they become interesting. They are, or become, individuals with problems; they lead lives of their own. This is of course a praiseworthy phenomenon in literature, but in the present case it brings about a creative tension. Figures who lead lives of their own are difficult to reconcile with a commentary on an age seen from a particular point of view. They are independent of and no longer subordinate to this point of view; they are often in conflict with the ideas which the author advances about their environment. Such persons can, and in Musil's novel do, reflect these ideas and their environment on a higher plane, but this reflection becomes very ambiguous. One can no longer say that Ulrich, Agathe, Clarisse, and Walter are what they are *because* of the period in which they live; would they be any different if the action of the novel had taken place in 1813 instead of 1913? Rather it is what they are or become that is important for the world of the novel; the major characters fit the setting, but they are not cut to measure for it. While the reader is often unclear about the nature of the intrinsic relationship of character to setting in the work, the tension often evident between the two seems to be one of the novel's great strengths.

Like the protagonists in *The Visionaries*, the characters in *The Man without Qualities* always speak the truth to each other as they see it. Doubts about the nature of this truth, as in the cases of Arnheim and Meingast, are always indicated by the author; the characters themselves are utterly sincere. There are few dramatic subterfuges here, hence little suspense of a conventional kind. As has been mentioned previously, few of the characters are described physically. The reader is left with a distinct impression of their relative sizes and shapes (Ulrich is tall and muscular, Clarisse is small and wiry, Diotima is round, Stumm is short and fat), but he has no idea of what their faces look like. Also, they speak for the most part in language heavily laden with metaphysically abstract terminology and indulge in philosophical speculation in the most incongruous settings, such as Diotima's boudoir, in a streetcar or on an outing. Ulrich's second mistress, whom he baptizes "Bonadea," is one of the few figures whose speech is drawn from life. The contrast between her and the others is in this respect marked.

In addition, the characters in this novel are passive; action is somehow made to seem irrelevant and trivial in this enormous talkfest, although there is enough of it to fill several conventional novels. Another, most important characteristic of the people in *The Man without Qualities* is that they are all deficient and incomplete. Individuals like Arnheim and Meingast, who claim to represent unities, are counterfeiters (in Gide's sense) from the point of view of Musil and Ulrich, coiners of false values. The incompleteness of these people gives rise to an interesting speculation: Are the character-pairs so prominent in the novel separate aspects of the same personality? I am referring not to the explicit case of Ulrich and Agathe, but to the subtler relationships of Moosbrugger to Ulrich, Soliman to Arnheim, and Rachel to Diotima.

It is perhaps appropriate here to make an observation of the greatest importance for an understanding of *The Man without Qualities*, an observation which has been touched on before without being made explicit. It concerns Musil's use of psychology. It can hardly be repeated too often that Musil was an experimental psychologist rather than a psychoanalytic one (since Freud has so completely conquered twentieth-century literature it comes as something of a shock to realize that there are other kinds of psychology). This can be empirically confirmed, aside from Musil's diaries, by considering any of Musil's figures. In the case of Bonadea's nymphomania, for instance, we do not explore its ultimate causes in her psyche but see manifestations of it in her relationship with Ulrich. In a discussion with Agathe on the concept of feeling Ulrich explains for Musil his neglect of psychoanalysis:

As far as Agathe could see he had left psychoanalysis completely out of consideration, and at first she was surprised at this, for like all people who are stimulated by literature she had heard it spoken of more than the rest of psychology; but Ulrich said that he wasn't leaving it aside because he didn't recognize the merits of this significant theory, which was full of new concepts and had been the first to teach how to bring together what in all previous times had been accidental private experience; but he was omitting it because precisely in that which he was proposing its particular virtues would not show to advantage in a manner worthy of that brand of psychology's quite demanding self-awareness.[45]

This preference for experimental over psychoanalytic psychology, quite aside from Musil's professional training in the former, has a unique value in his novel, for it furnished the basis of a synoptic rather than an analytic approach to life. To make a crude distinction, psychoanalysis emphasizes cause and experimental psychology effect. Psychoanalysis, beginning in the present, seeks by going farther and farther back into the past to arrive at important causes underlying a present condition. Experimental psychology is rather directed immediately toward the present condition; and as effect is an environmental factor and cause a psychic one, the use of experimental psychology in literature would seem to have an advantage over the use of psychoanalysis. It would also seem that the psychology implicit in literature is experimental psychology; what are Balzac's *Cousin Betty*, Goethe's *Elective Affinities*, or Henry James's *The Ambas-*

sadors but, from a psychological point of view, studies of behavior? Musil differs from these writers in this respect only in that he writes as a trained psychologist. Experimental psychology may be, or seem to be, out of fashion in our psychoanalytic and psychoanalyzed age, but it cannot be dismissed out of hand. It is important to remember that the psychological world of *The Man without Qualities* is not the world of Freud.

III

There are in *The Man without Qualities* five characters who especially reward closer investigation. An examination of Ulrich, Agathe, Clarisse, Arnheim, and Moosbrugger will lend substance to what has gone before and provide specific points of comparison between this novel and Musil's earlier works.

Inevitably, much has already been said about the central figure of *The Man without Qualities*. I would like here to fill in the outline of his character and role in the novel and to offer a criticism of him from a broader perspective.

In the chapter in which Ulrich is introduced (and as has been mentioned he is presented as a possibilitarian and a man without qualities before he is introduced directly) it is made plain that Ulrich did not become a possibilitarian in response to the age, but was one by nature. As a child he had been dismissed from one school for writing in an essay on "Love of Country" that "God makes the world and while doing so thinks that it could just as easily be some other way." [46] Consequently a distinction may be drawn regarding Ulrich, a distinction that Musil himself never formulates clearly: Ulrich may be said to be a possibilitarian by nature, but he is a man without qualities as the result of the place and time in which he lives, which may be said to be without qualities in the same sense that Ulrich is. (The term "without qualities" is misleading, for Ulrich has many and estimable qualities, but something prevents his realizing them.)

The inherent tension between these two aspects of Ulrich's character leads to a problem which is central not only in this novel but in all Musil's other works as well: How far is an individual formed by innate qualities, and how far is he formed by his environment? In his earlier works, as I have shown, Musil favored the former idea; what happens to Törless, Claudine, Veronika, and Thomas happens to them because they are the kind of people they are. Environmental forces can only reveal their basic natures, not form them. In other words, they are given individuals who are placed in a variety of difficult situations. Ulrich would not have become a man without qualities if he had not been born a possibilitarian. In a sense even his later development in the novel is simply a further development in the same direction. Ulrich, in short, is not as far removed from Musil's essentially fatalistic conception of character as might at first appear.

This point may be illuminated from another side. Neither Törless, Thomas, nor Ulrich, Musil's "anonymous" heroes with only half a name, can be said to change in the course of the works in which they appear. Ulrich as we leave him in a final fragment, in which Musil considers having him live through the Second World War, is the stamped form in a later stage of unfolding of the child who wrote the possibilitarian essay.

The clearest outline and sharpest criticism of the character of Ulrich is given early in the novel by Ulrich's friend Walter—their curious friendship consists almost exclusively of hostility, especially on Walter's part—when he bursts out about Ulrich to his wife Clarisse:

"He is a man without qualities!"

"What's that?" Clarisse asked, with a little laugh.

"Nothing. That's just the point—it's nothing! . . . You can't guess at any profession from what he looks like [Walter continues], and yet he doesn't look like a man who has no profession, either. And now just run your mind over the sort of man he is. He always knows what to do. He can gaze into a woman's eyes. He can exercise his intelligence efficiently on any given problem at any given moment. He can box. He is talented, strong-willed, unprejudiced, he has courage and he has endurance, he can go at things with a dash and he can be cool and cautious—I have no intention of examining all this in detail, let him have all these qualities! For in the end he hasn't got them at all! They have made him what he is, they have set his course for him, and yet they don't belong to him. When he is angry, something in him laughs. When he is sad, he is up to something. When he is moved by something, he will reject it. Every bad action will seem good to him in some connection or other. And it will always be only a possible context that will decide what he thinks of a thing. Nothing is stable for him. Everything is fluctuating, a part of a whole, among innumerable wholes that are presumably part of a super-whole, which, however, he doesn't know the slightest thing about. So every one of his answers is a part-answer, every one of his feelings only a point of view, and whatever a thing is, it doesn't matter to him what it is, it's only some accompanying 'way in which it is,' some addition or other, that matters to him."[47]

This is the way Ulrich appears to an old friend. His view of himself, while more penetrating, is not essentially different, and Ulrich spends most of his time trying rather desperately to explain himself to others. At one point, just after he has finished chiding Gerda Fischl on her extremist friends, Ulrich tells her:

In my own way *I* am radical, and there is no kind of disorder I can stand less than the intellectual kind. I should like to see ideas not only elaborated, but also correlated. I want not only the oscillation but also the density of the idea. . . . You say that I only talk about what might be instead of about what ought to be. I don't confuse these two things. And this is probably the most anachronistic quality that one can have, for nothing nowadays is so alien to anything as strictness and the emotional life are to each other, and our exactitude in mechanical things has unfortunately developed to such a point that it regards its proper complement as being the inexactitude of life. Why don't you understand me? You're probably quite incapable of it, and it's perverted of me to take the trouble of confusing a mind like yours, which is so happily in harmony with the spirit of the age.[48]

Ulrich also explains a psychological aspect of his motivation when later in the novel he tells his sister Agathe:

If I am to experience something actively, it must happen as part of a context, it must stand under an idea. I prefer to have the experience itself already behind me, in my memory; the actual display of feelings in it seems to me unpleasant and ridiculously out of place. . . . I have never stood under a lasting idea. . . . There hasn't been any. One must love an idea like a woman. Be blissful when one returns to it. And one always has it in himself! And seeks for it in everything outside himself! I've never found such ideas.[49]

Ulrich not only prefers thought to experience, he also uses thought as a defense mechanism against experience; like the woman who witnessed the traffic accident at the opening of the novel, Ulrich is often guilty of quickly systematizing potentially dangerous experiences in order to deflect their impact. He does this most notably as the drift of his relations with Agathe becomes clear to him.

Ulrich does not stumble into his role as Musil's representative of the man of intellect in the modern world. He is not the unaware uncomprehending victim of mysterious forces that Kafka's heroes are, although he shares with them a profound feeling of futility and frustration; indeed in his clear, articulate grasp of his own situation he is the opposite of the dimly aware heroes found so often in modern literature (Leopold Bloom, Willy Loman), although he is as passive as they. Again the ambiguous question arises, is he passive because he is the kind of person he is or because of the period in which he lives?

Ulrich's basic motivation should not be overlooked. It has three stages, each of which beyond the first develops after the failure of the preceding one. These stages may be said to represent Ulrich's attempts in three different directions to find a place in the world. The first of these is explained in Book I, Chapter 9; Ulrich wanted to be an important man but did not know what one was or how to become one. His three attempts to find a career, as soldier, engineer, and mathematician, are expressions of this basic desire. It is at bottom the desire of a man of possibility to become a man of reality. Since, however, Ulrich is by nature a man of possibility, he cannot help abandoning his attempts to influence the world directly. When Ulrich turns away from the world, it is to undertake a search for moral values on a moral plane. This crisis occurs, significantly, after an interview with Arnheim in which the latter, the incarnation of worldly importance, offers Ulrich a position in his industrial empire.

This deflection of purpose leads to the second stage of Ulrich's motivation. Here his desire for greatness is replaced by a sense of mission to lay the foundation for a new morality based on "exactitude and soul" so that, as he puts it at one point, even people who do not go to church would know what they should do.[50] When the participants in the Collateral Campaign turn a deaf ear to Ulrich's proposals, he decides, although not immediately or directly, to search with his sister in space and time for the Shangri-La of the morality of the future. This third attempt also fails.

Three stages, three failures: in the material world, the social world, and the mystical world Ulrich cannot translate his desires into action, or find much response in others for the action he considers so urgently necessary. Ulrich's strong moral sense transforms him in all three of these stages into a prophet. He tries to reform a world which has grown much too complicated to heed a prophet's call. People who are preoccupied with sports or Galician oil fields are not prepared to carry out the Sermon on the Mount, as Ulrich sorrowfully realizes. As a prophet in this sense Ulrich corresponds to Hölderlin's Empedocles, who tried to convert the people of Agrigentum to his calling when they were not ready to be called. In Hölderlin's drama Empedocles jumps into a volcano to prove to the people the sincerity of his belief; as Hölderlin explains in an essay on the play, the age demanded a sacrifice. Ulrich too sacrifices himself in the attempt to improve mankind, although after the failure of his various missions he dangles like a tired puppet in the uncertain hands of his author.

But in one fundamental respect Ulrich differs from

Hölderlin's hero. While he possesses physical courage, Ulrich suffers from a psychological timidity that prevents him from acting on the principles he so laboriously constructs in the labyrinths of his mind. For instance, although he recognizes in himself fairly early in the novel a predisposition to crime, he is shocked and frightened when Agathe, in forging a codicil to their father's will, actually commits one. It is Clarisse, sliding down the bumpy mountainside at the bottom of which insanity lies, who pinpoints this timidity in Ulrich. We never go far enough, she says in a chaotic letter to him in which Ulrich and the murderer Moosbrugger are, significantly, jumbled together. "*The misfortune is our stopping at the next to last step!*" she writes, and a little later in the same letter: "Trains collide because the conscience doesn't take the last step. Worlds don't turn up unless one pulls them. More about this another time. *The man of genius has the duty to attack!* He possesses the uncanny power to do it!"[51]

If we regard Ulrich as a would-be prophet, his relation to the other figures in the novel becomes clear. From their point of view he is what they have in common; he is the link between them. From his point of view they are the raw material out of which and for which his new morality will have to be fashioned, and the endless metaphysical discussions which Ulrich has with most of the other characters in the novel might be regarded as the exhortations of an evangelist to unrepentant sinners. Ulrich's task is not an easy one; his utopian morality not only will have to convince but also will have to include such diverse types as the materialistic financial speculator Leo Fischl, his bitter daughter Gerda and her racist friends, the psychotic Nietzschean Clarisse, and the astute General Stumm von

Bordwehr. Perhaps it was the size of this task which led Musil to caution that "what I present in the novel will always remain utopia; it is not 'the reality of tomorrow.' "[52]

Ulrich fails, then, in three successive spheres and as a prophet. But as he does so he points out what is wrong with the world—its complete lack of a unified context and the consequent meaninglessness of all its details. Like Nietzsche and Pascal, Musil cleared the tangled woods of an imperfect world with a view to planting a geometrically laid out forest of trees. "Ancient dreams of mankind are being realized in our times," Musil told an interviewer in 1926. "That in the realization they have not completely preserved the aspect of the ancient dreams—is that a misfortune? For this too we need a new morality. Our old one won't do. My novel would like to provide material for such a new morality. It is the attempt at a dissolution and an indication of a synthesis."[53] If we overlook the intriguing idea that a *novel* can provide material for a code of morality, we must agree that Musil is much more successful at dissolving than synthesizing. The successive defeats of Ulrich, as he fails and withdraws again and again, are starkly drawn; Ulrich as a synthesizer of a projected new morality is a name smothered in a cloud of abstract arguments. It will be remembered that at the conclusion of *The Visionaries* Thomas, whose values and life have come crashing down about his ears, says that all that is left is something called the "creative condition." It seems to me that in spite of the larger scope of *The Man without Qualities* Ulrich ends in approximately the same position as Thomas. The Phoenix is burned, and much is expected from the ashes.

I have said that Ulrich's failures are starkly drawn. The

point is worth pausing on because the moments of crisis in which Ulrich realizes his failures are among the most powerful moments in the novel. In them Musil has broken through the charmed circle of abstraction which, as I have argued, he set up in order to keep his characters (and perhaps himself) detached from his material. I would single out two such moments of crisis as being of the first magnitude.

The first and more sustained occurs in Book I, Chapters 116 through 122 (the conclusion of the second part of the novel). The Collateral Campaign has reached a point at which it is becoming apparent that there is no way to reconcile the conflicting ideas coming in from all sides. Ulrich suddenly sees that his life consists of the two separate trees, violence and love. Ulrich is here suffering from great mental fatigue, apparently due, although Musil does not say so explicitly, to his realization that the Collateral Campaign is a failure. This is the context in which Ulrich bursts out to the surprised Count Leinsdorf with his idea of a new task for the Collateral Campaign, that of founding a Global Secretariat of Exactitude and Soul.

In the following chapters Ulrich becomes more pensive and emotionally upset. A mob, aroused by rumors concerning the Campaign, storms the palace of its leader, Count Leinsdorf. It is Ulrich who faces this mob, which is perhaps symbolic of his own state of mind. As he watches the milling crowd, Ulrich mentally resigns from the Collateral Campaign and the world it represents. He is tired of thinking and wants to act. The very next chapter (121) gives him an opportunity to do just this; the Prussian industrialist Arnheim, toward whom Ulrich has been unremittingly hostile, offers him a high position in his far-flung empire.

Ulrich's reactions are complicated, but culminate in a feeling of loneliness. He tells Arnheim that he will think the offer over. Arnheim, who expected a refusal, is vexed.

In the final chapter of the second part (122) an abyss opens for Ulrich. He loses the sense of his personality, of his identity; walking home from the interview with Arnheim he "feels that a person was a phenomenon in this world; something that has an effect larger than it itself is." [54] The sights and sounds of the city are now dead for Ulrich; even as he thinks of the "law of narrative order" discussed above, this idea does not kindle him as ideas usually do. When he arrives home he finds a telegram announcing the death of his father, and as he prepares to leave Vienna Ulrich feels a change in himself in relation to his surroundings; he feels that his loneliness has become "ever thicker, or ever larger." [55] It seems to Ulrich that he has come full circle to where he was years ago, in his first and traumatic love affair with a "Frau Major," of which he thinks periodically throughout the novel. Ulrich then leaves for the station, and with this flight the second part of *The Man without Qualities* concludes.

The other important crisis in Ulrich's life occurs in the third part of the novel, on the island in the Adriatic to which Ulrich and Agathe have gone to consummate Ulrich's program for the realization of the millennium. Unfortunately the chapter in which it takes place, "The Journey into Paradise" (Book II, Chapter 94), exists only in the form of an early sketch, but it is clear that this was to be a major turning point in the work. This crisis also occurs at a moment of failure, when Ulrich and Agathe realize that their short period of mystic ecstasy as brother and sister and husband and wife cannot last.

These crises, then, are both associated with Ulrich's major failures. Except for them and a few less important places, Ulrich as a character is rather pale; he exists more as a tension between powerful forces than as the representation of a living human being. Is there not a conflict here between the fictional vehicle and the moral purpose of *The Man without Qualities?* A work of fiction, as I have argued, has a life of its own; a moral purpose does not. If a novel is used simply as a vehicle to present a moral purpose, or the search for one, many people are bound to feel that as a work of art it is deficient. One might argue that *The Man without Qualities* is strongest where Ulrich's preoccupations are most personal. Considering the work as a whole it is clear that the major part of it consists of a series of essays, and that characters and events tend to be incidental; in other words, that fiction is subordinate to idea. Musil says about this in "Thoughts for a Foreword": " 'superfluous,' 'long-winded' discussions: that is a reproach which has often been made against me, although the people making it might graciously admit that I 'could' tell a story. If only people would understand that to me these discussions are the most important thing!" [56]

The subordination of fiction to idea is most striking in the novel's central figure. The source of this important difficulty is worth indicating; it lies, I think, in the usurpation by the omniscient author as narrator of the role of the chief character. This destroys even the basic ironic situation for which I argued earlier in this chapter. For the ironic situation demands a careful separation of author and hero; confusion between them vitiates the character, as the author (who, after all, is writing the book) is invariably the stronger. The need for this separation does not seem to have been clear to Musil, for whom at least in this work a passion for ideas outweighed a passion for art. He himself expressed a lack of clarity in his conception of the respective roles of author as narrator and character as narrator in an undated paragraph on the "technique of narration," in which he wrote:

> I narrate. But this I is no invented character, but the novelist. An informed, bitter, disappointed man. I. I narrate the story of my friend Ulrich. But also what I have met with in other characters in the novel. This I can experience nothing, but suffers everything from which Ulrich frees himself and which yet destroys him. But without action, unable to come to a clear realization and activity which would correspond to the diffuse, unencompassable contemporary situation. [Narrated] with reflection from my standpoint. Narrated as by a last, wise, bitter, resigned survivor of the Catacombs.[57]

I would argue, then, that Ulrich's deficiency as a protagonist stems from two related things: a basic ambiguity in the author's mind between character as idea and as individual, and a lack of separation between the author as narrator and a character as a stand-in for the author. Proust, by placing the whole burden on his character in a roughly similar situation, by making his central character the narrator, avoided this confusion. Proust's asides as author are like small gems set in the ring of narration. Musil's essays are the ring in which too often characters and incident are set like small gems.

If this is the case, why did Musil write a novel at all? Why does a man whose chief concern is a moral one choose to embody his ideas in a work of fiction? The question is not a negative one, for I think *The Man without Qualities* offers a very positive answer to it. Morality is a theoretical concept; a novel is a picture of everyday life, or what could be everyday life, and at the same time the creation of a new life. If a man is passionately concerned with discovering a new morality for living, what is more logical than to throw theoretical principles into conflict with the life of sleeping, waking, and daily rounds which must be transformed? Writing a book of essays in the manner of Pascal and Nietzsche is not the important thing, Musil seems to be arguing; important is the prophetic impulse in which thought confronts life and attempts to conquer it, and the best place for such a confrontation is precisely the novel.

Like the central figures in all Musil's works except *The Confusions of Young Törless* and "Tonka," Ulrich finds himself in the situation of Dante, lost in a dark wood in the middle of life's journey; and except that the relativity of science has in our time removed the fixed spheres and circles through which man journeys to God, and indeed has removed God himself, Ulrich's progression in *The Man without Qualities* may be seen as a search for faith in some ultimate, all-encompassing unity which for Dante was embodied in God. But Ulrich's "journey" is more vital than Ulrich is, while the modern reader of the *Divine Comedy* finds that journey vital because the character Dante is. Ulrich rather belongs in the company of the Hollow Men of T. S. Eliot: "Shape without form, shade without colour, / Paralyzed force, gesture without motion."

But what is perhaps the basic criticism of Ulrich's passivity and withdrawal from life was made in 1759 by Samuel Johnson in *Rasselas*. "While you are making the choice of life," the philosopher Imlac tells Rasselas, "you neglect to live." [58] This penetrating comment leads us further into the most fundamental irony of Musil's novel. Ulrich takes a year's leave from life to choose how he may most effectively live, but the choice is not his to make. His fate is not in his hands but in his character, and his character reflects, but can hardly be said to arise from, the kaleidoscopic bits and pieces of cosmopolitan Europe before the First World War. *The Man without Qualities* trails off into side paths, falters and stumbles just as its "hero" does; and here, I think, may lie a key to it all. For this novel is not the story of its central character, but the book itself is, in a sense, its own subject. It falters the same way Ulrich falters, while Heartbreak House, drawing closer month by month to August 1914, draws closer to the edge of its own doom.

Agathe is the last of the major characters to be introduced (at the beginning of the third part), and she is distinctly subordinated to Ulrich. She both reflects and complements him; at first figuratively and then literally Agathe plays Eve to her brother's twentieth-century Adam—the conscience-stricken, post-Eden Adam. This comparison indicates the area of Agathe's problem in the novel: how to preserve her own identity in the face of the stronger masculine personality of her brother. In this she is a further development of Claudine in Musil's early story "The Completion of Love."

Ulrich is five years older than Agathe. They had been educated separately—Agathe in a convent, Ulrich in exclusive foreign schools—and have not seen each other for five years when their father's funeral calls them home to the provincial city of B (presumably Brünn, where for many years Musil's father was professor at the Technical University). The description of this city offers rich comparison and contrast to the description of Vienna at the beginning of the novel, and like the backgrounds of *The Confusions of Young Törless* and *Three Women*, this city contains a mixture of cultures. On his way there Ulrich remembers that Agathe had married while he had been abroad, and that her young husband had died a year later. (Agathe carries his picture in a locket around her neck; later she replaces the picture with a capsule of poison.) Three years after this Agathe had married again. This situation, and especially Agathe's attitudes toward her husbands—she loved her first husband and reveres his memory, but cannot stand her present one—are a repetition of the situation and attitudes of Regine in *The Visionaries.*

For Ulrich, Agathe's major importance lies in the sense of identity which he feels with her. She is the only human being in his life who seems to reflect the peculiar waves which he is always emitting to the world outside himself. This feeling of oneness between brother and sister is established at their first meeting in the novel. Each puts on, unknown to the other, an identical bizarre outfit, "large, soft wool pyjamas, . . . almost a kind of Pierrot costume." [59] Agathe's first words to Ulrich are: "I didn't know that we were twins!" [60] A short time later Ulrich notices the similarity of their faces as Agathe enters the room: "He felt that it was he himself who had come in through the door and was walking up to him: only more beautiful than he was, and sunk in a splendor in which he never saw himself. For the first time the thought seized him that his sister was a dreamlike repetition and alteration of himself." [61] On a later occasion Agathe asks Ulrich if he is familiar with the Platonic myth of the division of an original whole Man into Man and Woman (in the *Symposium*). Ulrich says yes, and adds: "But no one knows which of the many halves running around is the one he's missing." [62] He also reminds Agathe of the myths of Pygmalion, Hermaphroditus, and Isis and Osiris. Ulrich feels that part of Agathe's attraction is hermaphroditic, a circumstance which also plays a significant role in *The Confusions of Young Törless* and in Regine in *The Visionaries* and Clarisse in the present work. Agathe proposes that they be a "Siamese-twin couple," [63] a proposal that charms Diotima and others in Ulrich's circle because of what they consider its appropriateness.

But beneath this feeling of unity there is in Agathe a strong subconscious countercurrent, an irritation of the same sort, as has already been indicated, that Claudine felt for her husband. In suggesting this deep feeling without trying to verbalize it Musil's superb gift for portraying female psychology comes into full play. Like Ulrich's severe depression at moments of crisis Agathe's irritation is brought out only indirectly in her actions and emotional attitudes. As Ulrich seeks to make her more and more a part of himself, Agathe struggles more and more violently to free herself from him. She does not have her brother's astounding power of abstraction, which usually keeps him safely removed from emotional shocks. Without this vital protection Agathe is driven to flight and several times seriously contemplates suicide.

There is, however, enough of Ulrich in Agathe so that she too is fascinated by the possibilities of the millennium which her brother offers her in the third part of the novel. Of the two, Agathe is distinctly the less bound by moral convention. She is the one who acts out what Ulrich thinks of as possibilities (which rather frightens Ulrich); it is Agathe who changes their father's will while Ulrich watches. We are told that in committing this forgery "Agathe was now in the act of quitting the province of moral enclosure and launching out into that boundless deep where there is no other resolution than whether one rises or falls." [64] Agathe sees this crime as a token of a mystical union with Ulrich; after this she might almost be said to seize the initiative in their search for Paradise.

Living in Ulrich's house the couple rise to a plane of exaltation, almost completely isolated from the busy city around them. From this house to the brief incestuous consummation of their odyssey in Italy and on an island in the Adriatic is only a step. When they realize their failure Agathe reminds Ulrich of a promise to commit suicide; although they decide not to kill themselves Musil was apparently of two minds about it, for two pages later a new tension appears in Agathe which Ulrich doesn't notice, after which she drops out of the novel.[65]

To have Agathe commit suicide would accord very well with both her character and her progression in the novel; but in a fragment Musil indicates a resolution completely out of character for Agathe, that she is to be reconciled to her husband but will seek a divorce. It must be emphasized that any conjecture as to how the novel was to be resolved is dangerous; there is no concrete indication of a line that the further careers of Ulrich and Agathe were to take, but rather, as I have argued, a confusion about the whole problem.

Another important aspect of Agathe's personality has to do with Musil's basically fatalistic conception of character. "Fatalism" might seem to be a strange word to apply to a woman who has progressed from a convent school to incest with her brother, but a fatality in Agathe is clearly indicated in the same indirect way as are Ulrich's depressions in crises and Agathe's irritation against Ulrich. (Perhaps this is what Musil meant when he wrote that "what the story of this novel amounts to is that the story that should be told in it isn't told." [66]) The most important evidence of this fatality is the kind of men that Agathe attracts. They are all the same type, and are all distasteful to her. They are a type we have met frequently before in Musil's works, the pedantic professor: the mathematics professor in *The Confusions of Young Törless*, Josef in *The Visionaries* and Dr. Apulejus-Halm in *Vinzenz*.

Dr. Hagauer, Agathe's husband, is as anxious to get her back—she takes refuge from him with Ulrich after her father's funeral—as Apulejus-Halm was to have Alpha back or Josef to have Regine; and Hagauer threatens Ulrich in the same way that Josef threatened Thomas. In satirizing Hagauer ("who knew at all times at what degree of the week and month he found himself in the sea of infinity" [67]) and his fellow pedants there is a relish evident in Musil's writing which does not seem to correspond to any part of his purpose. I think it is clear that entirely too much of *The Man without Qualities* is devoted to lengthy and irrelevant satire of extremely marginal figures, satire for its own sake. This is especially marked in the case of Dr. Lindner, another man of the same type, who comes upon Agathe as she is about to attempt suicide for the first time. Although he becomes her protector, Agathe's feelings toward him are a mixture of attraction and malicious ridicule—an extension of the feelings of Claudine vis-à-vis the Ministerialrat in "The Completion of Love." Later, when Agathe and Ulrich are on their island, another professor appears to pay court to Agathe. This one is an art historian. It seems to be Agathe's fate to be the flame that attracts this particular kind of moth.

In spite of the subtle and beautiful delineation of Agathe's psyche, worthy in every respect of comparison with Goethe's portrayal of Ottilie and Charlotte in *Elective Affinities*, Ulrich's sister led her author, it seems to me, upon many byways which pointed away from rather than toward his central purpose. "I had no friend," Musil wrote in an early study for the novel, "(the relationship to Walter is hardly friendly, the reader will say!). That is one reason for Agathe." [68] Granted that Agathe's presence in the novel is necessary, Musil's weakness for portraying the feminine psyche tends to distract the reader. For this weakness is the area of Musil's great strength as a writer; the result is that Agathe is a much more appealing figure than her brother Ulrich. And in art as in life theories tend to fade in the presence of an appealing woman.

What is Clarisse's function in *The Man without Qualities?* Principally, I would say, to present and represent the mental aberration of the age. Clarisse, like Ulrich, is seeking a code of values to live by. Like him too she tries to realize a higher vision of man's fate. But she does not have Ulrich's mental strength; her fanatic vision crystallizes not around what could be but what is or was, principally Nietzsche and the murderer Moosbrugger (whom Clarisse regards as a savior). Unlike Ulrich, whose search leads him to withdraw from the world, Clarisse seeks to change the world by direct action, culminating in her effecting Moosbrugger's escape from an insane asylum.

In fulfilling her function as a representation of the time,

Clarisse plays several roles in the novel. She is part of two important triangles, the clash between the members of which is one of the chief ways by which Musil indicates the bankrupt values of European civilization. One of these triangles is that formed by Clarisse, her husband Walter, and Ulrich; the other, that formed by Clarisse, Ulrich, and Moosbrugger. Clarisse is also the flaming exponent of Nietzsche in *The Man without Qualities*, and finally (and logically, since her semi-insane mind is representative of her time), Clarisse's insights into the world and into the other characters in the novel are exceedingly penetrating. Only the mentally unbalanced, Musil seems to be saying through Clarisse, can understand the chaos of the twentieth century.

These last two points perhaps deserve elaboration. The numerous references in Musil's diaries to Nietzsche, who is referred to more than any other person, indicate Musil's lifelong fascination with the philosopher, but his attitude toward Nietzsche's ideas contains the same mixture of attraction and deep suspicion which characterizes the attitude toward Nietzsche of Thomas Mann and many other Germans. For proof of this one need only point out that Clarisse, the fervent champion of Nietzsche, hovers on the brink of insanity. (Clarisse's espousal of Nietzsche was Ulrich's fault in a way, for he had given her the works of the philosopher for a wedding present.) That Musil has a conception similar to Nietzsche's of the need for destroying false existing values in order to pave the way for new and better ones has already been indicated. Clarisse shows the other side of the coin.

Clarisse, as has been mentioned, points out to Ulrich that

the misfortune of people in his situation is that they stop at the next-to-last step. Her sharp insight shows many such flashes of brilliance. At one point she sums up Ulrich with whimsical appropriateness as "an ice-skater who capriciously approaches and zooms away on a mental rink." [69] Her comment on the two-headed eagle, the symbol of the Austro-Hungarian monarchy, is classic. She says to General Stumm von Bordwehr, noticing the eagle on his sword, "But what is a double eagle? An eagle with two heads? But only one-headed eagles fly around in our world! I call your attention to the fact that you carry on your saber the symbol of a split personality! I repeat, General, all magic things appear to be based on primitive insanity!" [70]

Physically Clarisse duplicates Regine in *The Visionaries;* like her she is small, wiry, and boylike. But mentally Clarisse is both more unbalanced and more aggressive than Regine; Clarisse "reminded one less of a human being than of the meeting of ice and light in the ghostly loneliness of an Alpine winter." [71] The erratic but progressive deterioration of her mind marks her successive appearances in the novel. This deterioration is handled by Musil as a case study, although it is characterized by infinite subtlety. Even the roots of Clarisse's disease are indicated in the detailed presentation of her family background.

Like many of the other persons in the novel, Clarisse had a model in real life, and to judge by several entries in Musil's diaries Clarisse is modeled after "Alice" with great precision.[72] I would like to submit that a conflict arises between Clarisse's function as a literary character, Musil's presentation of her as a case study, and the fact that she is a portrait drawn from life. These elements tend to pull in different directions rather than to be integrated with each other; the result is that Clarisse as a character is rather blurred in a way that Regine, in Musil's play, is not.

There is, however, one side of Clarisse's character which is compelling. This is her demonic activity. She and Agathe, the semi-insane and the amoral, are the two active agents in *The Man without Qualities*, and they both transgress the laws and mores of society. When Clarisse is not physically battling her husband Walter, who wants from her a child she refuses to give, she is fighting Ulrich, toward whom her feelings are highly ambivalent; when not doing that she is fighting her way into an insane asylum to see Moosbrugger, who seems to her to be an incarnation of Christ and Nietzsche. As Agathe drags Ulrich into crime in the forgery of their father's will, Clarisse drags Ulrich into crime in enlisting his aid in "springing" Moosbrugger from the asylum. Ulrich's passivity in both cases succumbs to the driving activity of the women; he is an implicated bystander at the opening of both of these Pandora's boxes.

Agathe and Clarisse are Pandoras of the mind, and this may be said to be their ultimate significance for Ulrich. They unlock the compartments in the brain of love and irrationality, releasing genies which overwhelm both Ulrich and themselves.

"I don't know what Hannibal looked like," Musil mused in his diary on January 11, 1914, after a detailed description of the Prussian industrialist, popular philosopher, and later German Foreign Minister Walther Rathenau (1867–1922), "but I thought of him." Already in this entry Musil mentions Rathenau as a model for his "great financier." [73]

The "great financier" in the novel is of course Dr. Paul

Arnheim. He has several functions: to show a false reconstruction of the decayed moral values of the age and at the same time to embody in his popularity and material success all those values held by the age; to epitomize the hollowness of the Collateral Campaign, with which he is intimately if unofficially connected, and to act as an antagonist to Ulrich. Aside from these more or less integrated functions there is another aspect that tends to usurp them; this is Musil's merciless satire of Arnheim's (Rathenau's) ideas.

It has already been mentioned that Arnheim is a coiner of false values in Gide's sense of the term. He sees in the modern world the same problem Ulrich sees, the widening gap between the material and the spiritual spheres, but his ideas about solving them are superficial. In seeking to guide the Collateral Campaign along the lines of his ideas Arnheim may be sincere; but the Austrians mistrust him because he is a Prussian. They are upset by the conflict between their patriotic sentiments on the one hand and the magnetic power of Arnheim's money and industrial might on the other. His sincerity is later put in doubt by General Stumm's revelation to Ulrich that Arnheim is chiefly interested not in the Collateral Campaign but in the Galician oil fields—a Shavian situation indeed.

Arnheim is a dilettante rather than a thinker. He can refer flippantly to "our spiritual bankruptcy"; [74] he uses the term "soul," for Ulrich so mystically charged, as a word rather than as a concept. His fine words are only a garment through which at times one can see the ruthless materialist underneath, as when he remarks to Ulrich that "the button one presses is always white and lovely, and what happens at the other end of the wire is someone else's business." [75] Arnheim is basically an empty man who mouths words and ideas he has picked up from the empty values of the society he wants to improve. They are consequently the words and ideas that comfort people and find a wide following; they are the words and ideas that people want to hear. At one point Arnheim is cruelly presented by Musil through the use of mechanical imagery: "Arnheim smiled, he made conversation. His lips played incessantly up and down in the sunlight, and the lights in his eyes changed like those on a signalling steamer." [76]

It is quite appropriate that this empty man should fall in love with his feminine counterpart Diotima, the vague guiding light of the vague Collateral Campaign. Between them they sum up much of the hollowness of thought about the basic problems of the age in ruling circles of society. But it is as an antagonist to Ulrich that Arnheim's presence in the novel really makes itself felt. Here are two men faced with the same problem; one of them has found a facile solution to it, the other none at all. But Ulrich, while he finds no solution, is at least, according to Musil, searching in the right direction.

In the charged interview between Arnheim and Ulrich their relationship comes to a head. Ulrich had previously expressed a dislike not for Arnheim personally but for what he represented. Arnheim's thoughts about Ulrich all revolve around the fact that there is something lacking in him, but Arnheim considers Ulrich an object of importance. Arnheim has the intuition about Ulrich that "this man possessed as yet unconsumed soul." [77] It becomes very important for Arnheim to control somehow this man with whom he feels some sort of identity and whose admiration he wants. In Book I, Chapter 121, Ulrich meets Arnheim alone at Diotima's, and Arnheim springs a Shavian surprise on him.

He offers to create for Ulrich a position in his industrial empire of General Secretary—a rather different kind of secretaryship from that of Ulrich's ideal of Exactitude and Soul. Shortly after making this offer to absorb the man of intellect in the materialistic maw of technology, Arnheim regrets his action; he thinks: "What will happen if this man accepts?"[78] In the tension that follows Ulrich gives no definite answer, although for him to accept is manifestly impossible. The offer is the trigger that sets off in the following chapter Ulrich's first major crisis. Being brought face to face with the shallow values he is seeking to overcome, and which seek to overcome him, strikes deep in Ulrich.

Arnheim, then, is Ulrich's most formidable antagonist outside himself. For unlike the crackpot philosopher Meingast (presumably a caricature of Ludwig Klages), a pseudo-Nietzschean activist who hovers around Clarisse, Arnheim has both weight and power. Meingast means little or nothing to Ulrich, but Arnheim means a great deal; he is the most significant representative in *The Man without Qualities* of the world as it is. Ulrich, trying to create a world that ought to be, finds that he cannot cope either with Arnheim or with the world Arnheim represents.

In an article that appeared in the magazine *Pan* in 1911, "The Indecent and Sick in Art" ("Das Unanständige und Kranke in der Kunst"), Musil argued that "in truth there is no perversity or immorality which would not, so to speak, have a correlative health and morality," and offered as an example: "It will have to be acknowledged that a sex murderer can be sick, that he can be healthy and immoral, and that he can be healthy and moral; in the case of murderers these distinctions are made." [79] One of the major problems connected with the figure of Moosbrugger in *The Man without Qualities* is: In which of these categories does this murderer belong? In other words, how responsible is he for his actions? A society that is none too healthy itself is embarrassed by this question and hence is uncertain what it should do with Moosbrugger.

Moosbrugger weighs on the conscience of society as he weighs upon that of Ulrich and in a different sense on the mind of Clarisse. It is doubtless no accident that Moosbrugger's first name is Christian or that he is a carpenter by trade (Clarisse is quick to draw the obvious conclusion) or that Ulrich feels a responsibility to help save him. But the figure of Moosbrugger is so ambiguously presented that any clearly symbolic interpretation of his character is impossible. His symbolic importance lies rather in what he means to the other individual characters in the novel, that is, in their interpretation of him.

The most striking of Moosbrugger's qualities is the discrepancy between his quiet, modest appearance and the violence of his crime, and also that between Moosbrugger's view of the world and the world's view of Moosbrugger. "To the judge, Moosbrugger was a special case; to himself he was a world, and it is very difficult to say something convincing about a world." [80] Perhaps it is this that first fascinates Ulrich about the man when he is present at Moosbrugger's trial and condemnation to death.

Ulrich's fascination with Moosbrugger is another evidence of that fascination of the rationalist with the irrational which is one of Musil's trademarks, and which might even be called the underlying theme of all his literary works. During his first major crisis, as he is walking home from his climactic interview with Arnheim, Ulrich is accosted by a prostitute. The turn of his thought is so involved, and so significant, that it is worth quoting at length:

And while he had been speaking to the girl, an obvious association of ideas had reminded him of Moosbrugger—Moosbrugger, the pathological play-actor, the pursuer and destroyer of prostitutes, who had walked through that disastrous night just as Ulrich was walking through this night now. When the street, the house-fronts, had ceased to sway like stage-scenery, remaining steady for a moment, he had run into the unknown being who had been waiting for him by the bridge, that night of the murder. What a wonderful anagnorisis that must have been, a shock of recognition rippling from the crown of the head to the soles of the feet! Ulrich felt it for a moment in his own body. . . . Evidently he had for so long kept to a life without inner unity that now he was even envying a madman for his delusions and belief in his role! But, after all, Moosbrugger was fascinating not only to him but to everyone else as well, wasn't he? In his mind he heard Arnheim's voice asking: "Would you set him free?" And he heard himself answering: "No. Probably not."

"A thousand times no!" he added, yet at the same time felt, like something suddenly dazzling him, the image of an act in which the movement of reaching out, as it springs from extreme excitement, and the being moved by it both fused into one in an ineffable communion in which pleasure was indistinguishable from compulsion, sense from necessity, and the highest possible degree of activity from blissful passive receptiveness. Fleetingly he recalled the view that the unfortunate beings afflicted by such states are the embodiment of repressed urges common to all, the incarnation of everybody's mentally committed murders and violations done in fantasy. Well then, let those who believed themselves justified in doing so deal with him in their own way, let them try him and condemn him, and so re-establish the balance of their morality, after he had served his purpose and satisfied their urges by his act!

The split in him was different; it lay precisely in the fact that he repressed nothing and so could not help seeing that what the murderer's image faced him with was something no stranger, or any less familiar, than any other image in the world, and every one of them was just like his old images of himself: half of it sense, consolidated, and half of it nonsense, dissolving, oozing out again! A rampant metaphor of order: that was what Moosbrugger was for him! [81]

"A rampant metaphor of order," "an intellectually emotional goal," "exactitude and soul"—Moosbrugger rejoins the root from which Musil's thought seems to have sprung, a passionate desire to find a rational order which could reconcile the forces of chaos.

IV

Looking at *The Man without Qualities* as a whole one is struck by a discrepancy between the avowed moral purpose of the novel and the novel itself. This discrepancy is both expressed and partly covered by the extensive autocriticism of the work, which is perhaps unequaled in modern literature. The novel contains at some point or other criticism not only of its method, object, subject and characters, but also of the values held and represented by the characters themselves and by the author. Characters such as Diotima, Walter, and Meingast, as well as Ulrich, Agathe, Arnheim, Clarisse, and Moosbrugger, are so thoroughly dissected from a critical point of view in *The Man without*

Qualities itself that to discuss them is often merely to simplify and repeat what is perfectly clear and often scintillating in the novel itself.

But this autocriticism does not remove a certain weakness from the novel. Basically this work is three things: a gallery of types of people, the portrayal of a society and of an age, and a primer of a new morality for mankind. It might be argued that these three levels are never quite integrated, and that as the book progresses they pull farther and farther apart. I have suggested that the lack of unity in this novel is itself an expression of the lack of unity of the world it portrays, and I think the novel has to be regarded in this light.

But one might also be more critical and argue that Musil did not know where his novel was going, and consequently let details run away with him. One might point out that there is in the work as a whole, unfinished though it is, a lack of proportion: not only numerous repetitive discussions, but also considerable duplication of characters—the latter an especially grave flaw in an author who regarded men as types. Instead of one caricature of a pedantic professor there are four (Schwung, a colleague of Ulrich's father, Hagauer, Lindner, and the art historian); instead of one facile popular philosopher there are three (Arnheim, Meingast, and the poet Feuermaul), and instead of one mistress for Ulrich we have two in succession (Leona, who seems superfluous, and Bonadea). These flaws cannot be denied.

But *The Man without Qualities* must ultimately be judged in other terms than these. It must be judged as an encyclopedic novel, a supernovel, and I would like to suggest that for this kind of work as sketched at the beginning of this chapter, integrated structure and symmetrical form are much less important standards than for the nineteenth-century novel written in traditional narrative form. If novelists such as Musil, Tolstoy, Mann, Proust, and Joyce reject this traditional narrative form of the novel as too limiting, the critic and reader must adjust their standards accordingly. Thus it would be wrong to maintain that *War and Peace* is a failure because it is not as tightly written as *Pride and Prejudice,* or that *Remembrance of Things Past,* for the same reason, is inferior to *Madame Bovary*. One of the tasks facing the critic of literature today is to find wider standards for judging these supernovels than those applied to the novel of the nineteenth century.

More than any other of the novels described in this chapter as encyclopedic, *The Man without Qualities* opens new perspectives on the limitations and possibilities of the human mind. In the last analysis, *War and Peace, Remembrance of Things Past, Ulysses,* and *The Magic Mountain* remain statements about life. *The Man without Qualities* is more than this. It is an open rather than a closed system of thought, a search on the border of the impossible for new directions of moral development. The basic moral question is how to live; this question is at the center of the work. The author's conception of his novel as a bridge being built out into space is a moral one; the ideal at the other end of the bridge is the right life. No other work of literature goes farther in laying bare for its readers the moral dilemmas of life in western civilization of the twentieth century. No other novel makes its readers aware to the same extent of these moral conflicts within themselves. The reader of Musil realizes that he is observing a radical, penetrating, surgical mind operating on a world which is only nominally that of yesterday. In reality it is the always timely world in which the individual seeks to formulate his uncertain relationships to himself and the society he lives in. In his search for a solution Musil set his gaze on the future rather than the past. While Thomas Mann stands at the end of an old tradition, there is reason to believe that Musil stands at the beginning of a new one. In any event the Rubicon between past and future has been crossed.

Notes

Chapter I: The Mind of Musil

1. Robert Musil, *Gesammelte Werke in Einzelausgaben*, ed. Adolf Frisé, III: *Prosa, Dramen, späte Briefe* (Hamburg: Rowohlt-Verlag, 1957), 387. Translations not otherwise credited are my own. The other two volumes of this edition are: I, *Der Mann ohne Eigenschaften* (1952), and II, *Tagebücher, Aphorismen, Essays und Reden* (1955). These volumes are referred to below as "*GW* I," "*GW* II," and "*GW* III." Scholars should note that the reliability and completeness of this edition have been widely questioned; see for instance "The Quality of Musil," *The* [London] *Times Literary Supplement*, No. 2,836 (July 6, 1956).

2. *Remembrance of Things Past*, trans. C. K. Scott-Moncrieff and Frederick A. Blossom (New York: Random House, 1927–1932), II, 1003.

3. *GW* II, 116.

4. *GW* II, 202, 203.

5. *GW* I, 610.

6. *GW* II, 92.

7. *GW* II, 810, 811.

8. *GW* II, 177.

9. *GW* II, 137.

10. *GW* II, 32.

11. *GW* I, 154.

12. *Ibid.*

13. In an interview granted the writer on November 12, 1956. See also Musil's appreciative essay of 1931, "Franz Blei—60 Jahre" (*GW* II, 767–771).

14. *GW* I, 1638–1639.

15. "Robert Musil," in *Deutsche Literatur im zwanzigsten Jahrhundert*, ed. H. Friedmann and O. Mann (Heidelberg: Rothe-Verlag, 1955), 339.

16. *Ibid.*, p. 352.

17. See *GW* I, 464–465, and *GW* II, 206–207.

18. See for instance the diary entry in *GW* II, 135–136 (quoted in Chapter V, p. 86).

19. "Über Robert Musils Bücher," *GW* II, 775.

Chapter II: The Fiction of Musil

1. *GW* I, 226.

2. *Maximen und Reflexionen*, in *Werke*, ed. E. Merian-Genast (Basel: Verlag Birkhäuser, 1944), XII, 40. Translation mine.

3. *GW* II, 136.

4. *GW* II, 146.

5. *GW* II, 808.

6. *Sonette an Orpheus*, I, 12.

7. *GW* III, 401.

8. *GW* I, 224.

9. *GW* II, 211.

10. *GW* I, 260.

11. *GW* II, 811–812.

12. *GW* II, 785.

13. *GW* II, 147.

14. *GW* II, 804.

15. *GW* II, 124.

16. *GW* II, 128.

17. *The Confusions of Young Törless*, trans. Eithne Wilkins and Ernst Kaiser (New York: Pantheon Books, 1955), p. 1.

18. *The Man without Qualities*, trans. Eithne Wilkins and Ernst Kaiser (New York: Coward-McCann, 1953–), I, 3. This translation, first brought out in England by Secker and Warburg, will be referred to below as "WK," followed by the appropriate volume and page number. As of the writing of this book only the first two volumes, out of a projected four, had appeared. Where this translation is used I also give the reference to the Rowohlt edition in parentheses.

19. *GW* I, 1636.

20. *GW* II, 478.

21. *GW* I, 40.

22. *Duineser Elegien*, VII.

23. *GW* II, 184–186, 197, and *passim.*

24. *GW* II, 140.

25. *GW* II, 197.

26. *Beitrag zur Beurteilung der Lehren Machs* (Berlin, 1908), p. 5. Discussing Mach's critics in an exposition of Mach's work, Hans Henning, in *Ernst Mach als Philosoph, Physiker und Psycholog* (Leipzig: Barth-Verlag, 1915), summarily dismisses Musil's thesis, which Henning claims is directed not against Mach but against Musilian bogeymen (pp. 183–184).

27. *Ibid.*, p. 15.

28. *GW* II, 869.

29. In an interview with the writer on Nov. 12, 1956.

30. *GW* II, 338.

31. *GW* II, 432.

32. *GW* II, 457.

33. *GW* II, 380.

34. *GW* II, 583. For the meaning of "Rapial" see *GW* II, 557.
35. *GW* II, 451.
36. *GW* II, 354.

Chapter III: The Confusions of Young Törless

1. *GW* III, 17.
2. *Ibid.*
3. *Ibid.*
4. *Ibid.*
5. *Ibid.*
6. *GW* III, 143.
7. *GW* III, 83.
8. *GW* III, 144.
9. *GW* III, 81.
10. *The Confusions of Young Törless*, p. ix.

Chapter IV: Unions

1. Munich: bei Georg Müller, 1911.
2. Cologne: Dumont- Schaubergschen Buchhandlung, 1907. The points in this paragraph are drawn from pp. 134–140.
3. In the interview referred to above.
4. *GW* III, 162.
5. *GW* III, 164.
6. *Ibid.*
7. *GW* III, 179. This passage can at best be rendered only approximately into English.
8. *GW* III, 191.
9. *GW* II, 811.
10. *GW* III, 166.
11. *Ibid.*
12. *GW* III, 174.
13. *GW* III, 192.
14. *GW* III, 199.
15. *GW* III, 182.
16. *GW* III, 199.
17. *GW* III, 206.
18. Here as elsewhere in this book I use the Freudian terms only for convenience.
19. *GW* III, 207.

Chapter V: The Visionaries

1. Ernst Heilborn, review of the first performance of *Die Schwärmer* at the Theater in der Stadt, Berlin, April 3, 1929, *Die Literatur*, XXXI (1929), 533.
2. *GW* III, 303.
3. *GW* II, 134–137, 145–146.
4. *GW* III, 303.
5. *GW* III, 305.

6. *GW* II, 810.
7. *GW* III, 303–304.
8. *GW* III, 324.
9. *GW* III, 307. Thomas uses the word "Geschwister." He is alluding to the fact that Maria and Regine are sisters.
10. *GW* III, 309.
11. *GW* III, 310.
12. *GW* III, 378.
13. *GW* III, 384.
14. *GW* III, 386.
15. *GW* III, 391–392.
16. *GW* III, 393–394.
17. *GW* III, 396.
18. *GW* III, 399.
19. *Werke*, XII, 22. Translation mine.
20. *GW* III, 393.
21. *GW* III, 401.
22. *GW* II, 135–136.
23. *GW* III, 337–338.
24. *GW* III, 305.
25. *GW* III, 342.
26. *GW* III, 306.
27. *GW* III, 315.
28. *GW* III, 368.
29. *GW* III, 373.
30. *GW* III, 395.
31. *GW* III, 401.
32. *Werke*, XII, 19. Translation mine.
33. *GW* III, 324–325.
34. *GW* III, 311.
35. *GW* III, 363.
36. *GW* III, 330.
37. *GW* III, 373.
38. *GW* III, 350.
39. *GW* III, 333.
40. *GW* III, 358.

Chapter VI: Vinzenz and the Girl Friend of Important Men

1. *GW* III, 440.
2. *GW* III, 425.
3. *GW* III, 427.
4. *GW* III, 412.
5. *Ibid.*
6. *GW* III, 444.
7. *GW* III, 433.
8. *GW* III, 419.
9. *GW* III, 441.
10. *GW* III, 444.

Chapter VII: Three Women

1. *GW* III, 229.
2. *Ibid.*
3. *Ibid.*
4. *GW* III, 236.
5. *GW* III, 230.
6. *GW* III, 239.
7. *GW* III, 240.
8. *Ibid.*
9. *Ibid.*
10. *GW* III, 243.

11. *GW* III, 247.
12. *GW* II, 186.
13. *GW* III, 249–250.
14. *GW* III, 257.
15. *GW* III, 260.
16. *GW* III, 262.
17. *GW* III, 263.
18. *GW* III, 264.
19. *GW* III, 265.
20. *GW* III, 298.
21. *GW* III, 267.
22. *GW* III, 268.
23. *GW* III, 269.
24. *GW* III, 279.
25. *GW* III, 283.
26. *GW* III, 289.
27. *GW* III, 291.
28. *GW* III, 293.
29. *GW* III, 299.
30. *GW* III, 278.

Chapter VIII: The Man without Qualities

1. WK I, 174–175 (*GW* I, 154).
2. WK I, 31 (*GW* I, 33).
3. WK I, 34 (*GW* I, 35).
4. WK I, 48 (*GW* I, 47).
5. New York: Viking Press, 1954, p. 54.
6. WK I, 257 (*GW* I, 224).
7. WK II, 174 (*GW* I, 456).
8. *GW* I, 1636.
9. WK II, 97 (*GW* I, 393).
10. WK II, 66 (*GW* I, 367).
11. Trans. Constance Garnett (New York: Halcyon House, 1940), p. 253.
12. *GW* III, 81.
13. *GW* I, 1648.
14. See "Nachwort des Herausgebers," *GW* I, 1661.
15. *Ibid.*, p. 1658.
16. See for example the article on Musil in *The* [London] *Times Literary Supplement,* No. 2,491 (Oct. 28, 1949).
17. *GW* II, 584.
18. WK II, 435–436 (*GW* I, 665).
19. "Nachwort des Herausgebers," *GW* I, 1658.
20. Trans. Edwin and Willa Muir (New York: Pantheon Books, 1947), p. 373.
21. WK I, 64 (*GW* I, 60).
22. *GW* I, 57.
23. *GW* I, 13.
24. WK I, 11 (*GW* I, 16).
25. WK I, 12 (*GW* I, 16).
26. WK I, 13 (*GW* I, 17).
27. *Ibid.*
28. Trans. Ronald Davis (Paris, 1925), p. 16; the preface, previously unpublished, is in French. Translation mine. While Ulrich is considerably more complex and more involved with the world than the distilled and disdainful M. Teste, they share a sense of

frustration and isolation and an overrefinement of the intellect, which M. Teste, however, has pushed to a logical conclusion.

29. WK I, 14 (*GW* I, 18).
30. *GW* I, 777.
31. *GW* I, 610.
32. V (May, 1923), 464. Reprinted in *GW* III, 597.
33. *GW* II, 355.
34. *Ibid.*
35. *GW* I, 1177.
36. *GW* II, 213.
37. *GW* I, 1644–1645.
38. Karl Markus Michel, in an article, "Die Utopie der Sprache" (*Akzente*, I [Feb. 1954], 23–35).
39. WK I, 300–301 (*GW* I, 260–261).
40. New York: Norton, 1951, p. 139.
41. Princeton: Princeton University Press, 1957, p. 42.
42. WK I, 231 (*GW* I, 201).
43. WK II, 275–276 (*GW* I, 539).
44. *GW* I, 43.
45. *GW* I, 1286.
46. WK I, 15 (*GW* I, 19).
47. WK I, 70, 71 (*GW* I, 65, 66).
48. WK II, 230 (*GW* I, 501–502).
49. *GW* I, 919.
50. *GW* I, 757.
51. *GW* I, 728, 729.
52. *GW* II, 378.
53. *GW* II, 788.
54. *GW* I, 662.
55. *GW* I, 679.
56. *GW* I, 1639.
57. *GW* I, 1635.
58. Ed. George B. Hill (Oxford: Clarendon Press, 1887), p. 108.
59. *GW* I, 690.
60. *Ibid.*
61. *GW* I, 709.
62. *GW* I, 923.
63. *GW* I, 928.
64. *GW* I, 814.
65. *GW* I, 1465.
66. *GW* I, 1640.
67. *GW* I, 967.
68. *GW* I, 1635.
69. *GW* I, 929.
70. *GW* I, 1224.
71. *GW* I, 360.
72. See for instance *GW* II, 125ff. Walter was similarly modeled on Alice's husband August ("Gustl").
73. *GW* II, 166.
74. *GW* I, 601.
75. *GW* I, 653.
76. *GW* I, 578.
77. *GW* I, 561.
78. *GW* I, 656.
79. *Pan* I (1910–1911), 309.
80. *GW* I, 77.
81. WK II, 438–439 (*GW* I, 667–668).

A Selected Bibliography

English Translations of Musil's Works

(The English translations of Musil's works are all by Eithne Wilkins and Ernst Kaiser)

The Man without Qualities. Vol. I, with a foreword by the translators, London: Secker and Warburg, and New York: Coward-McCann, 1953. Vol. II, London and New York, 1954. Vol. III, with a foreword by Eithne Wilkins, London, 1960.

[Note: The Wayne State University Press has announced for publication in 1963 the complete four-volume translation by Eithne Wilkins and Ernst Kaiser of *The Man without Qualities.* This edition will consist of a republication of the three volumes mentioned above and a fourth volume which will be translated into English for the first time and on the basis of a completely reconstituted German text.]

"The Perfecting of a Love," *Botteghe Oscure*, XVIII (Autumn 1956).

"The Portuguese Lady," *Botteghe Oscure*, XXV (Autumn 1960).

"Tonka," in *Modern Writing* [*The Avon Book of Modern*

Writing?], ed. W. Phillips and P. Rahv. New York: [Avon?], 1953.

Young Törless. With a foreword by Alan Pryce-Jones. London: Secker and Warburg, and New York: Pantheon, 1955.

Criticism in English

Boeninger, H. R. "The Rediscovery of Robert Musil," *Modern Language Forum*, XXXVII (1952), 109–119.

Braun, W. "Moosbrugger Dances," *Germanic Review*, XXXV (1960), 214–230.

——. "Musil's 'Erdensekretariat der Genauigkeit und Seele' —A Clue to the Philosophy of the Hero of *Der Mann ohne Eigenschaften*," *Monatshefte* XLVI (1954), 305–316.

——. "Musil's Musicians," *Monatshefte*, LII (1960), 9–17.

——. "Musil's Siamese Twins," *Germanic Review*, XXXIII (1958), 41–52.

——. "Robert Musil and the Pendulum of the Intellect," *Monatshefte* XLIX (1957), 109–119.

——. "The Temptation of Ulrich: The Problem of True and False Unity in Musil's *Der Mann ohne Eigenschaften*," *German Quarterly*, XXXIX (1956), 29–37.

"Empire in Time and Space," *The* [London] *Times Literary Supplement*, No. 2,491 (Oct. 28, 1949).

Kermode, F. "A Short View of Musil," *Encounter*, LXXXVII (Dec. 1960), 64–75.

Meyerhoff, H. "The Writer as Intellectual—*The Man Without Qualities* by Robert Musil," *Partisan Review*, XXI (Jan. 1954), 98–108.

Politzer, H. Review of *The Man without Qualities*, *Commentary* XVII (1954), 56.

——. "The Man without Qualities," *Books Abroad*, XXVIII (1954), 180–181.

Pritchett, V. S. "Musil, a Major Writer of Comedy in the

Viennese Manner," *New Statesman*, No. 47 (Apr. 3, 1954), 442–443.

——. "Translation of Robert Musil's Unfinished Novel *The Man without Qualities*," *New Statesman*, No. 45 (Apr. 11, 1953), 429.

Puckett, H. W. "Robert Musil," *Monatshefte*, XLIV (1952), 409–419.

"The Quality of Musil," *The* [London] *Times Literary Supplement*, No. 2,836 (July 6, 1956).

Criticism in German and Other Languages

BOOKS

Allemann, B. *Ironie und Dichtung.* Pfullingen: G. Neske-Verlag, 1956. (Contains a chapter on Musil.)

Arntzen, H. *Satirischer Stil: zur Satire Robert Musil's in "Der Mann ohne Eigenschaften."* (Bonner Abhandlungen 9.) Bonn: H. Bouvier, 1960.

Dinklage, K., ed. *Robert Musil: Leben—Werk—Wirkung.* Im Auftrag des Landes Kärnten und der Stadt Klagenfurt. Zürich: Amalthea-Verlag, 1960.

Lejeune, R. *Robert Musil, eine Würdigung.* Zürich: Verlag Oprecht, 1942.

Strelka, J. *Kafka, Musil, Broch und die Entwicklung des modernen Romans.* Vienna: Forum-Verlag, 1959.

ARTICLES AND DISSERTATIONS

Angelloz, J. F. Review of *The Man without Qualities*, *Mercure de France*, No. 318 (Aug. 1953), 709–712.

Bachmann, I. "Ins Tausendjährige Reich," *Akzente* I (1954), 50–53.

Baumann, G. "Robert Musil: Die Struktur des Geistes und der Geist der Struktur," *Germanisch-romanische Monatsschrift*, X (1960), 420–442.

Baumann, G. "Robert Musil, eine Vorstudie," *Germanisch-romanische Monatsschrift*, III (1953), 292–316.

Berghahn, W. "Die essayistische Erzähltechnik Robert Musils." Unpublished dissertation, University of Bonn, 1956.

Bertaux, F. Review of *The Man without Qualities*, *Nouvelle révue française*, XLI (1933), 300.

Blanchot, M. [Musil], *Nouvelle nouvelle révue française*, VI (1958), 301–309, 479–490.

Blöcker, G. "Robert Musil," in *Die neuen Wirklichkeiten: Linien und Profile der modernen Literatur*. Berlin: Argon-Verlag, 1957.

Boehlich, W. "Untergang und Erlösung," *Akzente*, I (1954), 35–50.

Fischer, E. "Das Werk Robert Musils. Versuch einer Würdigung," *Sinn und Form*, IX (1957), 851–901.

Friedrich, G. "Robert Musils 'Tonka,'" *Sammlung*, XV (1960), 652–659.

Kalow, G. "Robert Musil," in *Deutsche Literatur im zwanzigsten Jahrhundert*, ed. H. Friedmann and O. Mann. Heidelberg: Rothe-Verlag, 1955.

Kaiser, E. "*Der Mann ohne Eigenschaften:* Ein Problem der Wirklichkeit," *Merkur*, XI (1957), 669–687.

Knudsen, J. "Robert Musil, en intellektuel Mystiker," *Danske Magasin*, IV (1956), 465–479.

Luccioni, G. "La méthode de Musil," *Esprit*, (N.S.) XXVII (1959), 676–687.

Maier, A. "Franz Kafka und Robert Musil als Vertreter der ethischen Richtung des modernen Romans." Unpublished dissertation, University of Vienna, 1949.

Marko, K. "Robert Musil und das zwanzigste Jahrhundert." Unpublished dissertation, University of Vienna, 1952.

Michel, K. M. "Die Utopie der Sprache," *Akzente* I (1954), 23–35.

Müller, G. "Die drei Utopien Ulrichs in Robert Musils 'Mann

ohne Eigenschaften.' " Unpublished dissertation, University of Vienna, 1958.

Rasch, W. "Robert Musil und sein Roman *Der Mann ohne Eigenschaften*," *Universitas Litterarum*, IX (1954), 145–151.

Riskamm, K. "Robert Musils Leben und Werk." Unpublished dissertation, University of Vienna, 1948.

Rougemont, D. de. "Tristans neue Gestalt: Dr. Schiwago, Lolita und der Mann ohne Eigenschaften," *Der Monat*, XI (1959), 9–21.

Sokel, W. H. "Robert Musils Narrenspiegel," *Neue deutsche Hefte* VII (1960), 199–214.

Index

Balzac, Honoré de, 168
Blake, William, 131, 152
Broch, Hermann, 132, 139, 140-141, 157

Confusions of Young Törless, The (Die Verwirrungen des Zöglings Törless), 11, 18, 25-26, 41-56, 63, 80, 83, 116, 131, 132, 143, 157, 183, 184, 186
Cowley, Malcolm, 125

Dante, 181
Dostoevsky, Fyodor, 37, 129

Eliot, T. S., 13, 72, 163, 164

Flaubert, Gustave, 75
Freud, Sigmund, 39-40
Frye, Northrop, 160

Gide, André, 55
Goethe, J. W. von, 17, 18, 78, 80, 84, 90, 91, 149, 168, 187

Hamann, Richard, 59
Hemingway, Ernest, 104, 106
Hölderlin, Friedrich, 174-175
Hofmannsthal, Hugo von, 39, 72

James, Henry, 168-169
Johnson, Samuel, 181
Joyce, James, 29, 33, 61, 62, 119, 121, 134, 135, 152, 160, 198; *Exiles*, 73-74, 76, 82-83

Kafka, Franz, 25-26, 160
Kleist, Heinrich von, 145
Kraus, Karl, 10, 40

Mach, Ernst, 34-36, 59, 92
Maeterlinck, Maurice, 55
Man without Qualities, The (Der Mann ohne Eigenschaften), 3, 7, 8, 16, 21, 23, 26, 28, 29, 30, 34, 49, 50, 51, 53, 54, 60, 63, 64, 67, 69, 71, 76, 80, 81, 86, 91, 97, 99, 100, 101, 108, 117, 119-199; edition, 201; English translation, 207
Mann, Thomas, 10, 25-26, 119, 130, 134-135, 145, 152, 198, 199
Melville, Herman, 129-130

Nietzsche, Friedrich, 10, 125, 163, 188, 190

Plato, 151
Proust, Marcel (*Remembrance of Things Past*), 2, 119, 121, 134, 135, 198

Rathenau, Walther, 127, 190
Rilke, R. M., 10, 19, 31-32, 39, 69

Schnitzler, Arthur, 15, 61-62, 114
Shaw, Bernard, 91, 124
Stein, Gertrude, 33, 58, 62, 153

Stendhal (Marie Henri Beyle), 37, 38, 65, 121

Thoreau, Henry, 158-159
Three Women (*Drei Frauen*), 14-16, 102-118, 183; "Grigia," 14, 103-108, 143; "The Portuguese Lady" ("Die Portugiesin"), 14-15, 108-112, 143; "Tonka," 15, 112-117
Tolstoy, Leo, 198; *Anna Karenina*, 5; *War and Peace*, 119, 121, 134-135, 157
Trakl, Georg, 69

Unions (*Vereinigungen*), 12, 44, 57-70; "The Completion of Love" ("Die Vollendung der Liebe"), 12, 60-67, 75, 83, 186; "The Temptation of the Silent Veronika" ("Die Versuchung der stillen Veronika"), 12, 67-70

Valéry, Paul, 148, 205
Vinzenz and the Girl Friend of Important Men (*Vinzenz und die Freundin bedeutender Männer*), 13-14, 96-101, 186
Visionaries, The (*Die Schwärmer*), 1, 13, 19, 49, 54, 60, 71-95, 97ff., 116, 143, 183, 184, 186; first performance, 203

Wildgans, Anton, 40
Woolf, Virginia, 61, 62